The Story of Jesus
Is
Persistent Assumption

A Metaphysical Interpretation
of Scripture

From The Lectures Of

Neville Goddard

Unlocking The Mystery Of The Bible

Compiled
By
David Allen

Copyright © 2021

Copyright © 2021 by Shanon Allen / David Allen

All rights reserved. No part of this publication may be reproduced, distributed, or transmitted in any form or by any means, including photocopying, recording, or other electronic or mechanical methods, without the prior written permission of the publisher, except in the case of brief quotations embodied in critical reviews and certain other noncommercial uses permitted by copyright law.
Printed in the United States of America.

First Printing, May 2021

ISBN: 978-1-7370946-0-9

Visit Us At **NevilleGoddardBooks.com** for a complete listing of all our books and **1000's of Free (mostly metaphysical) Books to Read online and download.**

Copyright © 2021

Introduction

Please note that Assumption is just another word for Belief, which is another way of saying that what you say is true, is true for you. Belief is the law that brings our desires to fruition. Once you have decided what it is that you desire to be true, you live and move and breathe from that state of consciousness from then on. That is persistence. You need no objective proof that what you say is true, is true for you. The point of affirming your desire is that you are creating it in consciousness, not confirming an objective fact present to the senses, which is simply proof of past beliefs that have been brought to pass.

As Neville said . . "The most creative thing in us is to believe a thing into objective existence." If there is one thing to keep in mind as you study his works, it is just that, that we believe things into objective existence . . and the easiest way to do this is to simply construct sentences that imply that your desire is already fulfilled and BELIEVE THOSE WORDS.

As with all my books and compilations this book contains the very information that I have used in my own life to transform every aspect it. It is all about an inner transformation which results in an outer transformation with everything that happens in my life.

Having read Neville more times than I can count, I discovered there were several recurrent themes within all his teachings. Upon first reading them I wasn't aware of the simplicity of his teachings as I would come to see after many readings and years of study.

This particular book is one of the keynotes of his teachings. For without persistence in believing our desires are already fulfilled (already true) we will not see our desires manifested. We are always doing this whether we are aware of it or not. The difference is, by understanding the process we can do it consciously and not by default, which often ends with us manifesting unwanted conditions because we didn't realize the words we believe were becoming the conditions of our lives.

It is my hope and desire that I have complied his teachings in such a way that it makes it easier for anyone seeking the truth to not only find it but find it much quicker when you know what you are looking for before you begin reading.

"The Law of Life Is The Law of Belief." - Joseph Murphy

A few books that point to the power of our words creating our objective existence are Claude Bristol's "The Magic Of Believing", James Allen's "As A Man Thinketh", Napoleon Hill's "Think And Grow Rich", Wallace Wattles "The Science Of Getting Rich", Joseph Murphy's "The Power Of Your Subconscious Mind", Ernest Holmes "Creative Mind", Florence Scovel Shinn's "Your Word is Your Wand", Florence Scovel Shinn's "The Power of the Spoken Word", Frederick Bailes - "Basic Principles of the Science of Mind".

There are many others. These are a few suggestions.

David Allen

Contents

Excerpts from 68 Lectures . . Pages 7 - 94

       4 Complete Lectures . . Pages 95 - 133

There Is No Fiction . . 06-07-1968 95
The Secret Of Prayer . . 10-06-1967 105
Persistent Assumption . . 03-18-1968 112
Persistent Assumption . . 06-18-1968 119

Other books by David Allen 134

The Story of Jesus Is Persistent Assumption

A Metaphysical Interpretation of Scripture

The Story of Jesus Is Persistent Assumption

The story of Jesus is a persistent assumption that you are what you want to be, that things are as you desire them to be. This is true, for unless you believe that you are the being you now worship on the outside, you remain desiring and die in your sins of unfulfilled desires. You've got to begin to believe that you are Jesus Christ, the Word of God, which . . having gone out will not return empty, but will fulfill your purpose and accomplish that which you sent yourself to do. What is that? To fulfill scripture. That's all you are here for. On this level you can be rich if that is your desire, but remember the story of Jesus is persistent assumption.

(A Lesson In Scripture . . 10 - 23 - 1967)

Persistent Assumption

The story of Jesus is a complete and undeviating persistence in the assumption that you are what you want to be. If you haven't experienced wealth and that is what you want, persistently assume "I AM wealthy." If you have not experienced fame, assume you are famous, but "The day will come, saith the Lord when I will send a famine upon you. It will not be a hunger for bread or a thirst for water, but for the hearing of my Word." If that hunger hasn't come to you, then take the same story of Jesus and fulfill your every desire.

(A Lesson In Scripture . . 10 - 23 - 1967)

Persistent Assumption

"The story of Jesus is a persistent assumption." This is true in every aspect of your life. You want to be rich? That's the story of Jesus, which is a persistent assumption in the conviction that "I AM rich," for unless you believe that "I AM rich" you die in your sins and continue to claim "I AM poor." You want to be known? Then persistently assume: "I AM known." Want to be healthy? "I AM healthy!" Regardless of what you want to be, you must declare you already are it and persist in that assumption. An assumption is an act of faith, and without faith it is impossible to please God. Your reasoning mind may deny wealth. Your senses deny it too, but if you have faith you will dare to assume wealth, thereby becoming the man you want to be. Maybe, tonight you would rather continue to worship a Jesus Christ on the outside. Maybe you would rather continue to walk with the sheep of the world and not be the shepherd, but you would like to feed on green pastures by still waters, instead of climbing the steep hills of doubt and fear as most people do. You can, if you will persistently assume: "I AM well fed. I AM wanted. I AM known and everything is as I want it to be." But remember: to bring all these things into being, there must be a persistent assumption. That's the story of Jesus.

(Lecture - A Lesson In Scripture . . 10 - 23 - 1967)

Persistent Assumption

You who are here are hungry for the Word of God. You are thirsty for the Word of God. You could be at home this night watching TV and it would cost you nothing, but you have given up your time and your money to be here because of your hunger. I have been sent to tell you not only that you become God when he is fulfilled in you, but how to cushion the blows in this world of reason by delighting in his law. His law is simply a persistent assumption in the claim: "I AM what I want to be." Do not judge one who does not have the hunger for the Word of God, but tell him how to become what he wants to be.

Tell him that the story of Jesus is a perpetual, persistent assumption in whatever he wants to be. That Christ in him is the power of God and his imagination is that power and wisdom. Tell him that imagination knows how to bring his assumption to pass, but that he must persist.

Now I ask you: are you willing to persist in the assumption that you are what you want to be? Or are you going to go home tonight and say: "That was a nice little talk he gave, but after all he has a million dollars in the bank and I have nothing." If you think that, you are disobedient, for by that thought you have lack of faith in "I AM He!"

(Lecture - A Lesson In Scripture . . 10 - 23 - 1967)

Persistent Assumption

When I speak of Joshua or Jesus, I am not speaking of any historical creature, but the Christ in you who is the hope of glory! I am trying to get you to realize that Jesus Christ is in you as your own wonderful human imagination. So when I say: "God became Man that Man may become God" I mean: "Imagination became you that you may become all Imagination." Man has difficulty associating Imagination with God. Somehow the word "God" denotes some being that created the world, yet remained apart from it, but when I use the word "Imagination" it is my hope that the separation ceases to be. May I tell you: the whole vast world is all imagination. Our realists think they are nearer to the truth, yet they do not realize they are dictating nothing more than their imagination. They laugh at those who are mystically inclined, but may I tell you: leave them alone and go your way in confidence that what you are imagining you already are, you will become.

You imagined yourself into the state you are now occupying, and you can imagine yourself into any state you desire to express. No outside deity moved you into the state of misery you are now expressing; you did it yourself because you forgot who you are. You are the being who conceived every state in the beginning and deliberately started your journey by moving into a state, for you are Jesus, the Lord.

When I speak of Jesus, I am not speaking of some holy person as the world calls holy. The true story of Jesus is not as the churches teach. Their teaching is as far removed from the truth as Dante's "Inferno" is from The Sermon on the Mount. Dante had the capacity to spin beautiful worlds together, but what a state he fell into when he wrote his words. He was supposedly writing scripture and that is what the churches follow, yet it is so completely different from the real, true story of Christ.

Jesus is the very being of everyone in the world. The word "Jesus" means "Jehovah saves," and there is only one savior. Jesus is He who fell and He who saves himself. No one else saves you. You are saved by your own being. Becoming aware, you begin to remember; and remembering, you turn around and come out of the very play in which you sent yourself. And in the end all are united to form once again the single being that fell. The Lord God Jehovah, containing all, fell into diversity. In the end not one will be lost, but all will be gathered into the unity that is the Lord Jesus Christ. That is the story.

(Lecture - A Movement Within God . . 10 - 16 - 1967)

Persistent Assumption

If you want your dream realized, imitate God by becoming totally possessed by your dream. Do this and you, too, will reach your desire's fulfillment, just as God has brought . . and is bringing . . his dream to completion. Have an intense wish. Clothe it in tones of reality and imitate God by living as one possessed by a dream. Like God, do not turn aside until you have executed and accomplished the intents of your mind.

God began the good work in you and when he brings it to completion on the day of Jesus Christ, you will reflect the glory of God and bear the express image of his person. If God will not stop until that wish is completely realized, then you must be equally persistent. Regardless of things to the contrary, persist until your dream is completely realized.

The Story of Jesus Is Persistent Assumption

(Lecture - Be Imitators Of God .. 10 - 21- 1968)

Persistent Assumption

To say: "I AM going to be rich," will not make it happen; you must believe riches in by claiming within yourself: "I AM rich." You must believe in the present tense, because the active, creative power that you are, is God. He is your awareness, and God alone acts and is. His name forever and ever is "I AM" therefore, he can't say: "I will be rich" or "I was rich" but "I AM rich!" Claim what you want to be aware of here and now, and .. although your reasonable mind denies it and your senses deny it .. if you will assume it, with feeling, your inward activity, established and perpetuated, will objectify itself in the outside world .. which is nothing more than your imaginal activity, objectified. To attempt to change the circumstances of your life before you change its imaginal activity, is to labor in vain. This I know from experience. I had a friend who hated Roosevelt, yet wanted him to change. Every morning while shaving, my friend would tell Roosevelt off. He found great joy and satisfaction in this daily routine, yet could not understand why Roosevelt stayed the same. But I tell you, if you want someone to change, you must change your imaginal activity, for it is the one and only cause of your life. And you can believe anything in if you will not accept the facts your senses dictate; for nothing is impossible to imagine, and imagining .. persisted in and believed .. will create its own reality.

Now, all things exist in God, and he exists in you and you exist in him. Your eternal body is the human imagination, and that is God Himself. Your imagination is an actual body in which everything is contained. When you imagine, the thing itself comes out of that divine body, Jehovah. The story of Jesus is a wonderful mystery that cannot be solved until you discover, from experience, that he is your own wonderful human imagination.

The Story of Jesus Is Persistent Assumption

We are told that God speaks to man in a dream and unveils himself in a vision. Now, vision is a waking dream like this room, while a dream occurs when you are not fully awake. A few years ago this vision was mine: I was taken in spirit into one of the early mansions on 5th Avenue in New York City at the turn of the century. As I entered, I saw that three generations were present and I heard the eldest man telling the others of their grandfather's secret. These are his words: "Grandfather used to say, while standing on an empty lot: `I remember when this was an empty lot.' Then he would paint a word picture of what he wanted to build there. He saw it vividly in his mind's eye as he spoke, and in time it was established. He went through life in that manner, objectively realizing what he had first subjectively claimed."

(Lecture - Believe It In . . 10 - 6 - 1969)

Persistent Assumption

Now, in this world a man who wants to be a success in business can sit down and map out a pattern (a scene) which would imply he has the success he desires. Then if he enters the scene and believes its truth, the pattern of success will unfold and the world will confirm it. But he must persist in the image of success, just as God has persisted, for the day will come when God will awaken and express the success he believes himself to be.

(Lecture - A Prophecy . . 12 - 16 - 1968)

Persistent Assumption

There is no restriction placed upon the power of belief. There is no need to first consult some holy man to see whether you should have it or not. You be the judge. Choose your desire and, to the degree that you are self-persuaded that you have it, you will get it. And, because we are all one, if it takes one million people to aid the birth of your assumption, they will do it, without their knowledge or consent, so you don't have to ask anyone to aid you. They will do it not even knowing that they are. All you are called upon to do is to assume that you have it. An assumption, though false, if persisted in will harden into fact. That is the principle.

(Lecture - All That Is Divine . . 6 - 16 - 1969)

Persistent Assumption

If the world responds to your imaginal activity, is the world not David doing your will? If the Lord claimed that David always does his will, and you, by a simple imaginal act, command the outer world to respond . . are you not the Lord? When you imagine something it is as though you struck a chord, and everything in sympathy with that chord responds to bear witness to the activity in you. If the world is the responding chord to what you are imagining, and David is a man after your own heart who will do all your will . . is David not the outer world? This is not "will" as the world uses the word. You do not will something to be so, but imagine it and become inwardly convinced that it is so. And if, through your persistence, the world responds, you have not only found David, you have found the Lord as your own wonderful human imagination.

(Lecture - All That You Behold . . 4 - 19 - 1969)

Persistent Assumption

If you would like to live in a lovely apartment, claim you do. You may think you can't afford the one you want, but that thought is an imaginal act. I would suggest, instead of thinking you can't afford it, to simply sleep in that apartment tonight mentally, accepting the fact that you have all the funds necessary to pay for it.

The Story of Jesus Is Persistent Assumption

Persist and the world will respond. You will get the money needed to live there. The world does not cause, it only responds to your imaginal acts, for only God acts and God is in you as your own wonderful human imagination. Now, before you judge it, try it. If you do, you cannot fail, and when you prove imagination in the testing, share the good news with your brothers. Tell everyone you meet how the world works. You do not have to have a proper educational or social background to apply this principle; and you cannot fail, for an assumption, though false, if persisted in will harden into fact.

When you know what you want, assume you have it. Believe your assumption is true. Look at your world mentally and see your fulfilled desire. Do this and you are calling forth a response to your thoughts, and in the not distant future you will find yourself physically occupying the state imagined. Now, after you realize your desire, don't go back to sleep and hold on to this dream that is now solidly real, while trying to project a desire through secular means. We are warned against doing this in the parable of the rich fool, who said: "I have all that it takes, more than enough. I will pull down my barns and build bigger ones to store my grain and my goods. Then I will take my ease, eat, drink and be merry."

But the Lord said to him: "Fool! This night your soul is required of you." Don't hold onto anything on the outside; hold on only in your imagination. If something is taken from you, it is because at one time you assumed its loss and . . for a moment . . wondered what you would do if it were. You forgot the thought, but its message had already been released to fulfill itself. If you want to keep your possessions, you must hold onto them in your imagination and not build barns to house them.

(Lecture - All That You Behold . . 4 - 19 - 1969)

Persistent Assumption

Believe that all things are possible to you and that you are what you want to be. Persist in that assumption and it will harden into fact. Having assumed the life you now live, no one can take it from you but yourself! You have the power to lay it down by no longer being conscious of it, and the power to pick it up again through consciousness.

(Lecture - All Things Are Possible . . 11 - 3 - 1967)

Persistent Assumption

Tonight, when I leave this building I will ride home with my friend. As we travel we will pass certain streets and see familiar objects because we will be traveling by sight. But when I walk by faith my steps are invisible, for I will be walking in the assumption of my fulfilled desire. Paul tells us to "walk by faith and no longer by sight." We all know what it is like to walk by sight, but now we are called upon to break that spell and walk by faith.

I tell you it is possible to be anything you want to be, for the believer and the God of the universe are one. Don't divorce yourself from God, for he is your I AMness. Believe in your I AMness, for if you do not you will never fulfill your desire. Only by assuming you already are the one you would like to be will you achieve it. It's just as simple as that.

I am not saying it's easy, but it becomes easier with practice. If I gave a Stradivarius to one who had mastered the violin he could lift me to the nth degree of joy, but if I put the same violin in the hands of one who could not play it, he would shortly drive me insane. It's the same violin, yet one brings harmony while the other brings discord. You kill and make alive out of the same instrument, which is your own wonderful human imagination. You may make many discords until you learn how to play. We are here in this world of educated darkness learning to play the instrument which is God. You may not know anyone who would give you $10,000 right now, but if you believe all things are possible to God and you know that God is your human imagination, you can imagine you have the money, persist in your belief and you will have it. How, I do not know; I only know that according to your belief will it be done unto you.

Do you believe that all things are possible to God? And do you believe that he is your own wonderful human imagination? Knowing that God is all love, and you are capable of imagining unlovely things, you may not believe your imagination is God, but if that is true then God is not all-powerful. If you can imagine something that God cannot, then you transcend him. If God strikes only harmonious notes and you can strike chords that produce discord as well as harmony, then you are greater than he because you can do something he can't. But I tell you: your own wonderful human imagination kills and makes alive, it wounds and heals, for all things come out of the human imagination. While learning to use and believe in your human imagination you may make alive that which you do not want. You may wound yourself in the process, but what you create in your imagination you can uncreate.

Everything can be resolved, even though while learning, horrible mistakes are made. Don't condemn yourself for anything you have ever done, are doing, or may do, as you learn to play the instrument who is God himself and your own wonderful human imagination, for there is no other creative power.

(Lecture - All Things Are Possible . . 5 - 12 - 1969)

Persistent Assumption

Right now you are playing a part. If you don't like it you can change it. You could play the part of a man wealthier than you were twenty-four hours ago. It's only a part for you to play, if you desire it.

Everything I am telling you is from the Bible. "I kill and I make alive. I wound and I heal and there is none that can deliver out of my hand. I, even I AM He and there is no God besides me. I AM the Lord your God, the holy one of Israel, your Savior and besides me there is no savior." These are the words of God, revealed through his prophets of old. Their prophecy is fulfilled in the New Testament as: "Whatsoever you desire, believe you have received it and you will." That's how easily you apply it, for an assumption, though false and denied by your senses, if persisted in will harden into fact.

(Lecture - All Things Are Possible . . 5 - 12 - 1969)

Persistent Assumption

The ideal you serve and hope to achieve is ready and waiting for a new incarnation, but it is incapable of birth unless you offer it human parentage. You must assume that you already are what you hope to be and live as though you were. You must know, like Dr. Millikan did, that your assumption, though false to the outer world, will harden into fact by your persistence. The perfect man judges not after appearances, but judges righteously. He hears what he wants to hear and sees only the good. Knowing the truth that sets him free, he is lead to all good.

Character is largely the result of the direction and persistence of voluntary action; therefore, think truly and your thoughts shall the world's famine feed. Speak truly and each word shall be a fruitful seed. Live truly and your life shall be a great and noble creed.

(Lecture - Arise . . Date Unknown)

Persistent Assumption

I invite you now to go all out and imagine you really are the man or woman you want to be. But do not doubt, for the minute doubt steps in, a mental division descends, as doubt is the devil. If you will believe that regardless of what the world tells you, you are the man you want to be, you won't go mad. Instead, you will become that man. Your dream world will rearrange itself to fit your new image into it without any difficulty or help on your part.

When someone born into poverty persists in dreaming he possesses great wealth and his dream comes true, his wealth seems perfectly natural to those who do not know his dream. You are dreaming. If you try to make your dream come true while doubting its possibility, you are heading toward a nervous breakdown. But if you go all out in your wonderful claim, you will fulfill it, for all things are possible to the God you are, for you are the God of whom the Bible speaks.

(Lecture - Awake, O Sleeper . . 1 - 8 - 1968)

Persistent Assumption

Whatsoever you desire, ask in my name, for name simply means nature. If I wanted to be in a house and to feel that I am the occupant of that house, there is a certain feeling, a certain nature that goes with it. I must appropriate it as though it were true. Here I am called upon to bring something alive out of a state that is dead. For if I told you what I have done, you would question my sanity and you would feel I am trying to give expression to something that is being pulled out of nothing.

For you cannot see it . . you don't see me in the house, you don't see me actually occupying and enjoying the life that you know I desire to enjoy. So if I persist in that assumption, to you (if you should know my persistence) you might think I am headed towards a form of insanity. But if tomorrow the house becomes an embodied fact and I the occupant, then you look at it passively and you will still try to justify it by tracing its appearance back to a visible cause. You will see that in some way, unknown to you, my resources were lifted up, that in some way I became more eligible for that house and you will trace it back to a change in my fortune. You will trace it back to a change in something in my world, but you won't trace these changes back to the unseen assumption in which I dwell.

(Lecture - By Water And Blood . . 6 - 24 - 1956)

Persistent Assumption

You can put God to the test, and if He proves himself in the testing then you will know God is your own wonderful human imagination. If you want the joy of marriage, a love affair, or a romance, you can test God by assuming the one you desire is with you now. And to the degree you persist in that assumption, it will be yours to experience. Do not be concerned as to how or when it will happen; simply persist in the assumption that it has happened, and when it does you will know who God is.

(Lecture - Christ Bears Our Sins . . 2 - 24 - 1969)

Persistent Assumption

Jesus tells the parable of the woman who comes to a constable who, although he didn't fear God or respect man, rose and gave her what she wanted because of her persistence. Her constant comments forced him to give her what she desired. The story is also told of a man who came at midnight wanting something to feed a stranger in his house. The man from above said, "It is late and my children are in bed and I cannot come down and open the door," but, because the man persisted, he was given what he wanted.

You may think there is no way out of your present turmoil, but I don't care how fixed that seeming turmoil is, if you persist and persist and persist, he who is from above has to come down and grant your request. Practice repentance on this side of the veil while the work is going on in a hidden manner on the other side, and the wall will become thinner and thinner until the shell is broken and Christ is born.

(Lecture - Christ In Man . . 10 - 17 - 1966)

Persistent Assumption

Tonight learn to fine-tune your imagination. Knowing the voice of your friend, tune him in. Determine the words you want him to say and listen carefully. Tune him in until his words are fine and clear, then believe you heard him. Think it really happened. If you will, it will come to pass. When, I cannot say, for every imaginal act is like an egg and no two eggs (unless they are of the same species) have the same interval of time for hatching. The little bird comes out in three weeks, a sheep in five months, a horse in twelve months, and a human in nine months. Your imaginal act has its own appointed hour to ripen and flower. If it seems long, wait . . for it is sure and will not be late for itself.

An imaginal act is a creative act, for the moment it is felt, the seed (or state) is fertilized. It will take a certain length of time to be born, so start today by assuming you are the man (or woman) you would like to be and let the people in your mind's eye reflect the truth of your assumption. Be faithful to your assumption. Persist in this thought, for persistence is the way to bring your desire to pass. You don't persist through effort or fear, rather knowing that your imaginal act is now a fact; wait for its birth, for it will come.

(Lecture - Christ In You . . 5 - 6 - 1969)

Persistent Assumption

If you test your creative power on this level, the statement: "Whatsoever you desire, believe you have received it and you will," will no longer be a great theory given lip service, but will be known from experience. Believe you are the man (or woman) you want to be. Catch the feeling that you have already arrived. Look at your world from that assumption, knowing its truth.

Now, believe your assumption has its own appointed hour to flower. Persist in your belief and no power on earth can stop it from hardening into fact. This is Christianity!

There is no limit to your creative power. The most horrible problem will be resolved if you will but conceive a solution in your mind's eye. Anyone can do it. It doesn't take an Einstein to imagine a problem is resolved. Do not limit your creative power by determining the ways and means for it to come about, for imagination has at its disposal ways that are past finding out.

Do not be concerned as to how, when, or where . . only the end. If you are in debt, what is the solution? That you win the lottery or an uncle dies and leaves you his fortune? No! The end is that you are debt free. How would you feel if all of your bills were paid? Assume that feeling and let imagination harden that feeling into a fact!

Every problem has a solution. Imagine the solution and assume it is true. What would you see and do were it true? How would you feel? Persist in that feeling and in a way no one knows the solution will come to pass.

There is nothing impossible to God, and God is crucified on you as your own wonderful human imagination! There never was another and there never will be another God, and all things are possible to him. If you can imagine the end, knowing all things are possible to imagination and remain faithful to that assumption as though it were true, imagination will harden into fact.

Remember, creative power will not operate itself. Knowing what to do is not enough. You, imagination's operant power, must be willing to assume that things are as you desire them to be before they can ever come to pass.

(Lecture - Divine Signs . . 5 - 1 - 1968)

Persistent Assumption

So, I tell you tonight, you take your dream . . your noble dream, not only for yourself, but for others. What do you want? Ask them. Now, don't argue the point, what do you want? Well then, in your mind's eye dare to assume that they have what at the moment their reason and their senses deny and everything about them denies; but you remain faithful to the assumption, and your assumption relative to them. Though false at the moment, if you persist in it, it will harden into fact. Now, you try it. I could give you unnumbered cases, but why repeat them over and over?

Every case history in the Bible has been repeated now for two thousand years, and they still hold up, but they are all to encourage man to test God . . to try him. "Come, test yourself and see." You are not asked to test another. In the 13th chapter of II Corinthians: "Do you not realize that Jesus Christ is in you? Test yourself and see, unless of course you fail to meet the test." Well, if you fail to meet the test because of doubt and lack of faith, well and good. You might go and say: "It doesn't work." It's perfectly all right. So, it doesn't work for you because you did not believe it. He puts no limit to the power of belief. "All things are possible to him who believes." So can I really believe at the moment that I am trying to believe, everything tells me it can't be done? Can I ignore the facts of life, and then persuade myself that it is done and live in the end as though it were true? I tell you: if you try it, you will be able to write me and give me fantastic stories.

(Lecture - Faith . . 7 - 22 - 1968)

Persistent Assumption

"All that I have done, you will do, and ever greater things than these you shall do", because "I AM going to send the Holy Spirit, and He will bring to your remembrance all that I have told you." "He will bring to your remembrance" . . the whole thing unfolds within you. And then, you will tell others, and they will see you in the role, with all its side issues. Then they themselves become witnesses to the Truth, and in them the whole thing unfolds. And eventually, everyone is the Lord Jesus Christ. So, in the end, there is nothing but God!

But while we are here, we can use the Law that was given us. It's a simple law, and it will not fail you. But you must believe in Him. And you cannot believe in the Lord Jesus Christ, believing in someone other than your own wonderful human imagination . . not the real Lord Jesus Christ. If you want results, believe in the true Jesus, and the true Jesus is your imagination. And all things are possible to the human imagination, therefore, all things are possible to Jesus Christ, So, imagine yourself (and you name it). Believe in the reality of what you imagine. Persist in that assumption, and that assumption, though at the moment that you made it, it is denied by your senses, if you persist in it, it will become a fact. It will actually harden into some objective state.

Now, you test Him and see if this is not true concerning the Gospel of Jesus Christ, Well, if it works that way, why then, who did it? Well, you can't deny you did it. Well then, "If all things are made by Him, and without Him not anything is made that is made," and you know honestly that you did it, aren't you Jesus Christ?

The Story of Jesus Is Persistent Assumption

If I now assume that I am elsewhere, and reason denies that I am, my senses deny it, my pocketbook denies that I could even make the trip; if all of a sudden things change and compel me to make the trip, and what I did in imagination I am then compelled to do in the flesh, and I find myself actually there in the not-distant future . . I didn't devise the means, I didn't build the bridge of incidents; I went across that bridge and I came to the point where I actually was in imagination prior to the physical trip . . well, then, who did it? Well, all things are done by Him and I remember what I did, and so memory doesn't tell me, I remember exactly what I did, and then here I now do it physically, well, haven't I found Jesus Christ?

So, when you read in Scripture, "I have found him" . . found what? "I have found him of whom Moses in the law, and the Prophets wrote," Jesus, the Messiah. Well, then, where is he now? Well, "Come and see." And then they went up unto the place, "and it was the tenth hour," and so they remained with him.

Now, the modern translation of the Bible tells us it was 4:00 o'clock in the afternoon. What nonsense! It hasn't a thing to do with any 4:00 o'clock in the afternoon. I know the day, in the Hebraic language, starts at 6.00 a.m., and it goes through, but, it isn't 4:00 o'clock in the afternoon. The Prophet meant exactly what he said when he said, "It was the tenth hour."

Well, in the language of the Bible these hours are significant, and "ten" does not mean four in the afternoon. "Ten" is the letter "Yodh," and the letter "Yodh" has the symbol of the hand. It's the creative hand, and the symbol is a seed; it's the creative seed. They speak of him as a carpenter. What is a carpenter? You and I think of a man with a hammer and nails, and he builds a house, or he builds a chair; he's a carpenter. Not in Scripture! A carpenter means "one who produces from seed," just as a mother, as a plant, as the earth, to be born, to be delivered, to bring forth, bringing forth from seed.

The Story of Jesus Is Persistent Assumption

Well, ten means seed, so, he was at the creative point, and they remained to learn the story of creation. So, they came to him, and because it was the tenth hour, they remained, and did not depart. And they say it's 4:00 o'clock in the afternoon! It hasn't a thing to do with any 4:00 o'clock in the afternoon! This comes to the point where now they are going to discuss the creativity of God. It is ten: the hour is ten. And here is the seed, and this is how it works.

What's the seed? Tell me what you want. That's a seed.

Well, how do I plant it?

How do you plant it? What would it be like . . what would the feeling be like if it were true that you had it? That's how you plant it.

Then I become a carpenter, and I build from scratch. I actually build from the seed, the seed being my desire, my hope, my longing. I assume that I AM what at that moment of assumption my reason and my senses deny. But I dare to assume it! Well, that's the carpenter. So, they went to the carpenter's house, and it was the tenth hour, and he shows them the secret of bringing things out as you would out of the earth, out of the woman, out of the plant. Well, there must be a seed there. The seed is your want, your desire.

And, so, in the modern version they have it translated into what is called the modern English and call it 4:00 p.m. or 4:00 o'clock in the afternoon. You will miss the entire mystery of Scripture if you start doing that with the words of Scripture. These meanings are unique, and they are forever. And you can't change them.

(Lecture - Family Portrait . . Date Unknown)

Persistent Assumption

Now I urge you to put his teaching into practice. He taught you to simply appropriate a subjective state which is your objective hope, and know it must externalize itself in your world. Do that and it will. Ask in faith, without a doubt, for those who doubt are like the wave of the sea that is driven and tossed by the wind. They are double-minded, for they know what they are while desiring to be something else. You must be single-minded by dropping what you believe you are and assuming that you are already what you desire to be, for you cannot desire something you already possess. Look into the wonderful law of liberty which sets you free, and you will see your freedom in the faces of your friends. Persist in your assumption and it must come to pass.

(Lecture - Feel Deeply . . 5 - 30 - 1969)

Persistent Assumption

We are called upon to exercise this power that sacrificed itself and became us. As Blake said: "I know of no other Christianity, no other gospel than the right, both of body and mind, to exercise the divine art of Imagination." By exercising the divine art of imagination, you can prove to yourself that you can go beyond what your eyes, reason, and senses dictate. Exercise this art by daring to assume you are what your reason and senses deny you. Persist, and to the degree you are self-persuaded of its truth, the outer world will change, for it is forever conforming to the belief housed within you.

(Lecture - Follow The Pattern . . 3 - 25 - 1968)

Persistent Assumption

You can be the man . . you can be the woman . . that you would like to be, but wanting it is not going to do it. You must be it. You can't just say, I would like to be it; you must assume that you are it, and sleep in the assumption that you are it, for the assumption, though at the moment denied by your senses . . denied by everything round about you, if persisted in will harden into fact. So, you dare to assume that you are the man . . the woman . . that you want to be, and day after day live in that assumption as though it were true, and that assumption will become a reality in the world. Even if you go hungry, it doesn't matter. No matter what happens, go hungry; but persist in the assumption, and that assumption will objectify itself and become a reality in your world.

(Lecture - God Given Talent . . 5 - 31 - 1971)

Persistent Assumption

On this level you can start from here, right now, and fulfill any dream. May I tell you: you are going to live the life that you are imagining, so imagine well! Imagine the most glorious thing in the world and . . no matter how wonderful it is . . may I tell you it is nothing compared to the being that you really are. Nothing in this world can come close to the being you really are. This world of Caesar is only a tiny section of your infinite being, but while you are here, dream nobly.

Dream lovely dreams, for you can realize everything if you are willing to imagine that you have them now. Begin now to imagine you are the man (the woman) you would like to be, and regardless of what happens tomorrow, next week, or next month, if you persist in the assumption that you already are that which you want to be, you will become it in this world of flesh and blood. Everything here will vanish, yes

. . but why not test your creative power? Then you will begin to taste the power latent within you, and you will discover that you can conjure out of your own depth things that are seemingly impossible, conjured by the mere act of assumption. If you dare to act and persist in acting as though it were true and it becomes a fact, then you will know the truth of your creative power.

(Lecture - God Is Light . . 10 - 9 - 1967)

Persistent Assumption

So, you look into your own minds eye and know exactly what you want in this world. When you know what you want in place of what you are, then you are seeing your savior, your Jesus. The story is, don't let Him go, but let all else go. Disengage yourself from the whole vast belief that you formerly entertained, and hold on in your imagination to the concept that you ARE the man that you want to be. That will lead you toward Calvary. Calvary means fixing in your own minds eye that state, and that will lead towards Easter or this wonderful day that we speak of as the Resurrection. For you will resurrect and make alive the state that began only as a concept. If you remain faithful to the concept you will be led right into the fulfillment of that state. It is called, in the Bible, rebirth.

Now here is the story. He said, "Except you be born again, you cannot enter the kingdom of heaven." The wise man said, "How is it possible a man my age may once again enter my mothers womb and be born again?" He said, "You, a master of Israel and you do not know? Except you be born of water and the spirit, ye can in no wise enter the kingdom of heaven." Then he gives this clue, "As Moses lifted up the serpent in the wilderness, even so must the son of man be lifted up." As Moses lifted up the serpent do you think a man lifted up a brazen serpent as told in the story and that everyone who looked on it was instantly healed and those who would not look were not cured? It's not any serpent. A serpent is a symbol of the power of endless self-reproduction. For the serpent sheds its skin, and yet does not die. Man must be like the serpent, who grows and outgrows. So I must now learn the art of dying that I may live, rather than, I would say killing that I may survive. I die, by laying down all that I now believe, and I lift myself up to the belief that I am what I want to be. That's how I do it.

Now this is how a man is born of water and of the spirit. If I told you now that an assumption, though false, if persisted in, will harden into fact, that is a truth, that is water. But water is not enough. You must catch the spirit of it and apply that truth. Well, if I know that if I assume that I am the man I want to be and persist in that assumption, I would gradually become that. If I have that knowledge, that's marvelous. But not to DO it is to try to bring this being to birth by water only. We are told this is the one who came by water and the blood. Not by water only, but by water and the blood. In other words, I have the knowledge, but I cannot bring to birth my ideal by bare knowledge. I must put it into action, I must DO it. Then when I DO it, I take my savior and I crystallize him by the doing. This is the story of our wonderful Easter.

(Lecture - Good Friday Easter . . Circa 1954)

Persistent Assumption

You can play any part . . be it a rich man or a poor man, a beggar or a thief, the known or unknown . . once you know they are only parts, only states of consciousness. But if you don't know this, and are not willing to give up your present state, you will remain there, looking at your desire and not from it. You can become what you would like to be in the twinkle of an eye by the simple act of assumption.

And the day you dare to remain faithful to your assumption, it will begin to externalize itself. And when it does you may return to sleep, just as you do in your night dreams.

Becoming possessed by the dream you created in your sleep, you observe your own creation; and if it is a noble dream, you can become so puffed up in your own concept that you forget its creator. Or you can create something ignoble and become so immersed in it you believe in its reality. Anything can be created by a mere assumption. When I dared to assume I was the man I wanted to be, I did not discuss it with others; I simply persisted in my assumption and watched it harden into fact. That persistent act taught me that this world was a dream.

(Lecture - I AM The Cause . . 10 - 19 - 1969)

Persistent Assumption

In the beginning of creation the Spirit of God (his creative power called Christ) moved upon the face of the deep. Now, motion cannot be detected save by change in position relative to another object. Unless there is a fixed reference from which an object moves, no movement will appear. Let us use a weak, sick man as our fixed reference and looking into our mind see a strong, healthy man, and say: 'I remember when he was weak and sick, but look at him now!" Do that and you have moved relative to the man.

Look at yourself in the mirror and dare to see radiant health and happiness reflected back to you. Then say within yourself: 'I remember when my reflection was so different." Persist in seeing your new image reflected there and you will resurrect that state. Your image, your concept of yourself or of another, is in your own wonderful human imagination who is Christ and Christ is the only God. God the Father and Christ your creative power are the same being, therefore he has never left you!

(Lecture - I Remember When . . 4 - 10 - 1968)

Persistent Assumption

To believe in anything outside of yourself as the cause of the phenomena of life, you are believing in something made with the human hands . . I don't care what you call it. Now, who is this God who does as He pleases that is equated with man? Well, you try to think of anything other than your wonderful human imagination!

"Our God is in the heavens," and we are told that, "Heaven is within you," in the 17th chapter of the book of Luke; "God is within you". If He is within me, what in me does anything that it pleases? Nothing but my imagination! I can imagine anything in the world. The most incredible thing, I can imagine, but as man, one condition is imposed upon me: I must believe it.

If I can persuade myself of the reality of that which I have imagined, no power in the world can stop it from coming to pass. Man creates his objective world out of imagination and faith. These are the substances out of which he actually projects and objectifies his world. There is nothing but God, and God is man's own wonderful human imagination.

"Man is all imagination; and God is man, and exists in us, and we in him." "The eternal body of man is the imagination, and that is God Himself." [Blake, from "Annotations to Berkeley" and "The Laocoon"]

So, Divine Imagining . . yes, it's instantaneous; but when it's keyed low into the human form, then there is one condition imposed upon it:

Can I believe it?

So, I now come to the point of faith. What is faith?

Faith is the subjective appropriation of the objective hope.

So, I have a hope. I would like to be this, that or the other in this world. Or, I would like someone . . a friend of mine . . to be this, that or the other. Now I must appropriate it subjectively. I go down in my imagination and I simply conceive a scene, which would imply that it's true, and I appropriate it.

How do I appropriate it? I create a scene, which would imply that it is true, bringing the individual or friends before me. I could have friends tell me, "Have you heard the good news?" and I will act as though I didn't.

"No, what is the good news?"

"Have you heard the news about ..." . . and they mention my friend, and I listen eagerly to what they are telling me about my friend. I am appropriating subjectively my objective hope.

All I have to do then is to persist in that state. As Shakespeare said in his "Anthony and Cleopatra":

"It hath been taught us from the primal state that that which is was wished until it were."

(Lecture - If You Really Can Believe . . 6 - 15 - 1970)

Persistent Assumption

So, everything in this world is possible. "All things are possible to him who believes." The only condition imposed upon man is: Can you believe it when reason denies it and your senses deny it? No limitation is placed upon God, "With God, all things are possible" . . no limitation. But God became man; and as man, He imposed upon Himself the limitation, and that limitation is belief.

Can you believe it?

The Story of Jesus Is Persistent Assumption

So, can you tonight believe that you are what at this moment everything denies? I don't care what it is . . can you believe it? Will you persist in that belief as though it were true, and walk tomorrow, though you haven't a thing to eat, just as though it were true? And persist in it. You don't have to raise a finger to steal anything in this world, or to do anything of which you would be ashamed. Just simply persist in the belief that you are the man . . the woman . . that you want to be. It will come to pass!

An assumption, though false, if persisted in, will harden into fact.

This whole vast objective world was produced by imaginal activities. I don't care what the world will tell you . . there isn't a thing you see now in the world that was not once only imagined. The clothes you wear, your haircut, the house in which we are now housed . . everything was once only imagined. And then it was persisted in, and it became a reality.

But then, you will say, "But after all, people did do it." I am not denying that. You don't have to build it. You hold the vision. And those who will build it, they'll build it, but you will own it. You will pay them their price . . pay them fully. They, too, can transcend their present position if they desire to be beyond what they are, but they must first want to be. And when they want to be and they wish it, they will go back to that primal state:

"It was taught us from the primal state that he which is, was wished until he were."

So, you want to be . . and you name it . . I won't tell you what to be. You name what you want to be. Now go beyond the things of Caesar. Would you like to be, beyond all things in the world, one who actually experienced the Gospel? That, too, is a wish. So, you can remain here forever building bigger and bigger and bigger things in the world.

(Lecture - If You Really Can Believe . . 6 - 15 - 1970)

Persistent Assumption

Your own wonderful human imagination is the actual creative power of God within you. It is your savior. If you were thirsty, water would be your savior. If you needed a job, employment would be your savior. Your imagination is the power to save you from whatever circumstances you now find yourself. You can experience your heart's desire through the use of your imagination. Nothing is impossible to your imagination. Your imagination is unlimited in what it can accomplish. If you can imagine something, you can achieve it. Let me give you an example. If you were unable to walk and were confined to a wheelchair, you could close your eyes and imagine yourself running on the beach or wading in the water. If you would imagine yourself doing this until it took on the tones of reality, you could accomplish a healing that would allow you to actually walk or run.

The way to use your imagination creatively is this. Relax in a chair or on a bed and close your eyes. First determine what it is you wish to experience. Then, in this state of complete relaxation, bring to mind the end result of what it is you desire. In other words, if you were seeking a promotion at work, the end result might be that people would congratulate you on your promotion. You might move to a larger office. You would enjoy an increase in pay. Take anyone of these events and, with your eyes closed, actually hear your friends congratulate you on your promotion. Feel their hand in yours as they tell you how happy they are for you. By actually feeling that you are being congratulated, your imagination will go to work to bring about that state in your outer world. You need not be concerned about how this will be accomplished. Your imagination will use whatever natural means are necessary to bring it about. "I AM the beginning and the end." "My ways are past finding out." What you do in imagination is an instantaneous creative act. However, in this three-dimensional world, events appear in a time sequence. Therefore, it may take a short interval of time to realize in the outer world what you have just experienced in imagination. After you have performed this act in your imagination, open your eyes and go about your normal, natural affairs, confident that what you have done must come to fruition in your world. Make your inner conversations conform to your imaginal act. You have planted a seed and you will soon see the harvest of that which you have sowed.

When you go into your imagination, make sure that you are actually performing the action, hearing the words, touching the object, or smelling the aroma in your self-conceived drama. What you do in your imagination is not merely a daydreaming which you see events in your mind's eye. You must enter the dream as if you were actually there. You must make "then" now and make "there" here. To make this perfectly clear, imagine that you would experience driving a new car after you have achieved your goal. In that case, you would not merely see a new car in your mind's eye. You must actually enter the dream. Feel yourself seated behind the steering wheel. Smell the newness of the interior. Feel yourself enjoying a comfortable ride. Feel the happiness that would be yours after accomplishing your dream.

That which you experience in imagination is an actual creative act. It is a fact in the fourth dimension of space and will make its appearance in this three-dimensional world just as surely as planting a seed will result in the growth of a particular plant. Once you have planted this seed in your imagination, do not uproot it by being anxious about how it will be accomplished. Each seed has its own appointed time. Some seeds take a few days; others a little longer. Feel confident that what you have planted will appear in your world. Your imagination will draw all that it needs to make your dream an actual reality. It if takes others to play a part in order to accomplish your end, your imagination will draw that person into your drama to play his or her part in the sequence of events. Your only responsibility is to remain faithful to your imaginal act until you experience it in your outer world. You can repeat your imaginal act each night before falling asleep. In fact, you may wish to enact this drama over and over again until it feels normal and natural to you as you drop off to sleep. Your imagination will work out the means to realize your dream while your conscious mind sleeps.

Bring your five senses into play as you perform your imaginal activity. Actually hear a friend's voice congratulating you or feel yourself hugging that person. If you wanted a new piano, run your hand over the smooth wood, touch the keys, and listen to the sound. If you wanted to receive a dozen roses, actually smell the fragrance and touch their velvety petals.

Finally, you must be persistent in attaining your desire. Continue to imagine what you want until you have actually obtained it. You do nothing else to obtain your desire. If it is necessary to take some action, you will be led to do so in a normal, natural manner. You do not have to do anything to "help" bring it about. Remember that it is God, Himself, who is doing the work and He knows exactly how to accomplish it. If you think of your desire during the day, give thanks that it is already an accomplished fact . . because it is!

Dream better than the best you know.

(Lecture - Imagination Creates Reality . . Date Unknown)

Persistent Assumption

When I was in my early twenties, I found myself in a situation that was very unpleasant to me and I wanted to get out of it. After attending a lecture by Neville, I waited to speak to him afterwards. I briefly told him of my unhappy circumstances and was hoping he would offer some advice as to how to change them. He smiled at me and said, "Don't accept it." At that time in my life I did not fully grasp what Neville had been teaching. I thought he had misunderstood my question, and I tried to clarify my problem by stating that I had already made the choice to be in the situation I now found so unpleasant. Neville again smiled and said, "Don't accept it." I left his presence quite frustrated, thinking he had not understood my problem. I continued to read the two

The Story of Jesus Is Persistent Assumption

books I had by Neville. I gradually understood that regardless of the circumstances which surrounded me, I did not need to accept them as final. I began to imagine what I wanted rather than focus my thoughts on my negative surroundings. An event took place two weeks after I began my imaginal acts that was instrumental in bringing about my heart's desire five months later . . that of a brand new home. Meanwhile, the situation that had been so depressing to me improved, and I spent the next five months planning what I would do in my new home.

Think about some past disappointment you may have had. Perhaps you were looking forward to attending a special event with someone. In your anticipation of it, did you think, "This is too good to be true, something will probably happened to spoil it." Something probably did happen to create conflict or to cause you to miss it entirely. Man finds it relatively simple to disregard the promise of something good by thinking of all the reasons why he cannot achieve it.

People around you may be quick to point out that you are being unrealistic when you mention a desire that appears difficult or impossible to reach. We should all be unrealistic in the face of the army of doubt if we would experience our wish fulfilled. We are called upon to disregard the ―facts‖ which would deny the achievement of our heart's desire. Habit is the only thing that keeps our thoughts moving along the old familiar negative ruts. No one can change your thought patterns and, therefore, your life but you. It is worth all the effort it may take to center your attention and feel as if you already possess that which you want in place of things as they are. Consciousness is the only cause and the only reality. Every negative experience was produced by first giving attention and feeling to that condition. What consciousness has made, it can unmake. Your responsibility is to impress upon your mind the change you wish to express. Your imagination is the creative power that can and will accomplish the end without effort and in a natural way.

Appearances confirm our former habitual patterns of thought. That which you imagine yourself to be today will project itself in your world tomorrow. Persistence in assuming that you are the person you wish to be, despite your present circumstances, is the only condition imposed upon you to embody that ideal.

(Lecture - Imagination Creates Reality . . Date Unknown)

Persistent Assumption

All of us are mentally speaking within ourselves every waking moment. Our inner conversations must match the wish fulfilled if we would realize our desire. If our desire is for a better job and we imagine ourselves being congratulated because we are gainfully employed in a wonderful position, we must also make our inner conversations conform to that end. We must be certain that we are not saying within ourselves something like, "That boss of mine doesn't believe in promoting people;" or "It would be difficult to find any job at my age, never mind a better one," or similar statements that would imply that we do not have that which we desire. We must persist in the feeling of our imaginal act by making our mental conversations conform to what we would say had we already realized our aim.

If, for instance, we wished to own a new car, we could imagine a new car parked in our garage or imagine ourselves driving it, or imagine our friends admiring it. We must then make our inner conversations reflect the type of conversations we would engage in were we really the owner of a new car. Our conversations could consist of discussing our new car with friends such as telling them of the wonderful fuel mileage we are receiving, or hearing our friends tell us how much they enjoy riding in our new car, etc.

Our inner conversations are just as creative as our deliberate imagining of the wish fulfilled. In fact, if they are of the opposite nature, they can negate what we have imagined. You must watch what you are saying internally to make sure that these conversations coincide with your wish fulfilled. If you become aware that these inner talks contradict what you would like to achieve, revise them so that they follow along the track that would indicate that you already have what you desire or are already the person you wish to be.

(Lecture - Imagination Creates Reality . . Date Unknown)

Persistent Assumption

I tell you: imagining creates reality. Believe me, for it is true. Fawcett was right when he said," The secret of imagining is the greatest of all problems to the solution of which the mystic aspires, for supreme power, supreme wisdom and supreme delight lie in the far off solution of this mystery.

A friend of mine sent Mr. Fawcett my book, and called his attention to the chapter called, "Revision". He also sent a copy to one who was a physicist at one of our great universities. The physicist felt that since the statements recorded there were not scientifically provable, the book was not worthy of his library. While the old gentleman . . who was a philosopher and teacher at Oxford University . . wrote the sweetest letter, saying: "I do not know who Neville is, but having read the chapter on revision as you requested, I know that he could only have received it from the brothers. No one but the divine society could have dictated this chapter." Here was a man filled with praise for a thought the scientist ridiculed because it was beyond his grasp.

I ask you to take me seriously. Imagination will fulfill itself, so do not limit yourself by anything that is now happening, no matter what it is. Knowing what you want, conceive a scene which would imply you have it. Persuade yourself of its truth and walk blindly on in that assumption. Believe it is real. Believe it is true and it will come to pass. Imagination will not fail you if you dare to assume and persist in your assumption, for imagination will fulfill itself in what your life becomes.

(Lecture - Imagination Fulfills Itself . . 10 - 26 - 1968)

Persistent Assumption

I urge you to dream nobly. Although your dream may seem impossible, invite it into your consciousness by feeling it is real. Wear this feeling as you would a suit of clothes, and persist until the feeling takes on the tones of reality. Do that, and in a way no one knows, your desire will appear as an eruption of your continuous thought.

Your desire started in motion when you wore it. Its appearance is simply a hidden continuity which came to the surface. Dwell upon a thought, and you will realize that it is not original. That the thought itself is complete and therefore every thought is Divine plagiarism!

Enter a mood and watch the thoughts that come to you while there. If you want to be known, get into the mood by feeling recognized as you move about. Then as the feeling becomes familiar you will be amazed how things will reshuffle themselves and you will get the publicity you desire. It may not be very flattering, but if you really want to be known, you will be.

"Whatever you desire, believe you have received it and you will." Knowing what you want, assume you have it and let no one divert you. Do your father's will, believing in the feeling of your wish fulfilled. Try it, for this simple principle will not fail you. But remember: you are its power, as it does not operate itself. I can tell you how to move into another state, but you must move into it. No one can do it for you. You see, states are permanent and it is up to you to get out of the state you are now in if it is undesirable to you.

(Lecture - Live The Answer Now . . 1 - 15 - 1968)

Persistent Assumption

You can sit quietly and enter a glorious dream. If it's shadowy, you are not in it. Persist until you enter it, and it will become the only reality. Live in the state of your fulfilled desire now, knowing that in a way unknown and unnoticed by you it will erupt to become an objective fact.

Take the challenge of scripture: "Whatever you desire, believe you have received it and you will." Dare to believe you have what reason and your senses deny. Persist in your assumption and it will harden into fact. Try it and see! And remember: the Father who became you is speaking to you through the medium of dream and revealing himself in vision, for this world is His play!

(Lecture - Live The Answer Now . . 1 - 15 - 1968)

Persistent Assumption

Man must be born from above or he cannot enter the Kingdom of Heaven. Everyone will be born from above, for that One to be born is already in man dreaming. The Dreamer-in-man is Jesus Christ. You are dreaming this world. Now dream it nobly. Dream noble dreams. All can come to pass.

In your dreams dare to assume that you are the man that you want to be. Assume that you are it, and persist in that assumption; and that assumption, in a way you do not consciously know, will harden into fact. All assumptions if persisted in become what the world calls 'reality'. So, do not give up. The most fantastic dream can become true if you assume it and walk in the assumption as though it were true.

Night after night, sleep as though you are the man . . the woman . . that you would be or that you would like to be.

And then, if tomorrow does not bring it to pass, it doesn't matter. There are intervals of time between the assumption and its fulfillment. It's like generation. So, if you dare to assume it, give it time. And then some bridge of incidents will be built for you without your conscious knowledge of it, and it will lead you across that bridge to the fulfillment of your assumption in a way that you do not know.

So, dare to assume a noble concept of yourself. Live in it as though it were true; and may I tell you? It will become true.

(Lecture - Neville's Purpose Revealed . . 6 - 25 - 1971)

Persistent Assumption

I am telling you what I know from experience and what is known from experience is known more thoroughly than any other way in this world. You may know something from hearsay, you may read it in a book, see it in a play, or hear it from the speaker; but you cannot know it in the true sense of the word until you have experienced it. When the dreamer in you begins to awake, then you realize that the world is a dream and you can prove it to yourself.

If this waking world is as much a dream as your sleeping world, you should be able to control it. In the dream of last night you might have been frightened and believed for a moment that the event was real, outside of yourself, and beyond your control.

Only when you awoke did you discover that it was a dream. Had you known at the time that it was a dream, you could have controlled it and made the event conform to your desire. Now awake in this world, you think it is real and outside of yourself, but I tell you: this world is a dream, too. It is every bit as much a dream as the dream of the night, only it is more difficult to control because it appears so real and independent of your perception. But it can be controlled by a simple act of assumption.

The Story of Jesus Is Persistent Assumption

Let us assume that this is a dream and everything is perfect. You are happy and content and all is right in your world. Then persuade yourself of the reality of your assumption. Don't do anything to make it so; just trust the dreamer in you to bring it to pass, for the power who assumed your desire is the Lord Jesus Christ, and all things are possible to him. Your assumption, though false in the sense that it is denied by your senses and reason, if persisted in will harden into fact in such a normal, natural way that you will think it would have happened anyway. That is the dream. When imagination fulfills itself so naturally, it is easy to question that your assumption had anything to do with it; but I tell you it could not have happened without your assumption, for your awareness is the one and only cause of the phenomena of your life.

(Lecture - No Other Foundation . . 10 - 10 - 1969)

Persistent Assumption

Believe me: your own wonderful human imagination is the one and only God, so put him to the test. Know what you want and let him create it for you. Search for and find the feeling that would be yours if things were as you desire them to be. Look at your world . . would you see it differently? Would those in your world see a different you? Create that scene, catch the feeling of reality and don't let go! Don't forget what you saw and how you felt, for he who creates in you must have a model to work with. Don't be the double-minded man Jesus speaks of: 'The double-minded man is unstable in all of his ways. He looks into the mirror of life and sees what he looks like, then he turns and forgets what he was like.'

Do not turn away from what you have just imagined and forget what you really look like, but persist in the new state. Remain faithful to it and let the one within you (who is Christ the Lord) externalize it, for you and He are one. I don't mean you and the Lord, but you are the Lord. There is only God in this world and you will know one day that you are He.

(Lecture - No Other God . . 5 - 10 - 1968)

Persistent Assumption

I refuse to accept the 'facts' of life unless they conform to the ideals that I want to enjoy in my world. So, I hear something of a friend of mine. He is unemployed. So, he's unemployed . . that's the fact. Well, am I really free? If I am really free from the 1739 tyranny of Egypt . . free from the house of bondage, having heard what I heard, I will now represent him to myself as gainfully employed. Now, the facts deny it, but I will remain faithful to my assumption as though it were true, confident that imagining creates reality, and therefore, if I persist in my assumption, it will harden into fact. Well, having done it and proved it over and over and over, having shared what I have discovered with others, to see them doing it over and over . . then you become indifferent as to what others think. If there is evidence for a thing, does it really matter what another think s . . if they tell you that you are stupid to believe that an imaginal act will harden into fact?

Well, having done it and proved it over and over and over, having shared what I have discovered with others, to see them doing it over and over . . then you become indifferent as to what others think. If there is evidence for a thing, does it really matter what another thinks . . if they tell you that you are stupid to believe that an imaginal act will harden into fact? You mean that you have nothing in this world . . but nothing! And you dare to assume that you have . . not only that you have, but you have what you want, and that others share it with you, and they know that you have it; and you'll sleep this night on an empty stomach in the belief that you've been well fed? That you sleep this night as though things were as you desire them to be, when every fact of life during the day denies it? Well, that's what we are called upon to do! We are called upon to trust Him . . to put our trust in Him. Who is He? My own wonderful human imagination! I don't say his imagination . . not his. "I AM" is his name. It's first person present, not "I was;" not, "I will be," but "I AM."

But suppose I have imagined it and it hasn't happened? Well then, what are you doing now, saying that I once imagined it and I am not still imagining it? In other words, if you call me by my name, you say, "Well, Neville", I'll respond. If I'm running away from something of which I am ashamed, I will still in some strange way show that I do respond to that name. Well now, I've put a name on "I AM." I AM . . and you name it: healthy, wealthy, known . . whatever it is you desire in this world. Why forget it. Why forget what you've put upon the name of God? For the name of God, and the only name of God, and the everlasting name of God is "I AM." He has no other name.

(Lecture - No Other Gods . . 7 - 16 - 1968)

Persistent Assumption

Tonight's subject is Power. I do not mean the power of Caesar, I'm speaking tonight of the power of God, for here in this world of Caesar I think all nations would admit that this land of ours is by far the greatest power in the world of Caesar: economic power and military power. And here we are, against a tenth-rate nation, and find on our hands the longest war in our history. We say we have an objective and that we have the means to achieve it, but we are unwilling to use the means that we have. Well, then, modify the objective to fit the means that we are willing to use. That belongs to the world of Caesar. If we do not modify the objective to fit the means we are willing to use, then cut bait and forget it, and forget the so-called 'saving face.' But I am not speaking of that kind of power. I am speaking of the power of God, which is called in Scripture, "Jesus Christ." Paul defines Christ as "the power of God and the wisdom of God." Here we find wisdom and power exalted and personalized as God's companion in the creation of the world. That power is your own wonderful human Imagination. That's the power of God! That is Christ. As far as I am concerned, that is Jesus Christ of the Scriptures.

Now, tonight we are talking about this power. The earliest gospel is Mark, and the first words we find on the lips of this power [are]: "The time is fulfilled, and the Kingdom of God is at hand. Repent, and believe in the gospel". Now, the word repent as we use it in the world is not what Scripture means when we use it here. We mean to feel remorse, regret. That hasn't a thing to do with the word repent. It's the Greek 'metanoia,' a radical, but radical, change of attitude, a radical change of mind.

Can I see an objective, and then everything tells me: well, I can't realize it? Well, do I have the power to realize an objective? I tell you, we have; we have the power. Well, what is the deeper meaning of power but effectiveness in achieving one's purpose in life! Well, so I have a purpose. Do I have the power? I tell everyone: Yes. You can imagine the end, can't you? Can you imagine what it would be like if it were true? Can you feel what it would be like if it were true? Well, then, that is power! Now, can you be persistent in it? Can you remain faithful to that end as though it were true?

Now, I don't care what the objective is. You have the power to achieve it if you know this power is the power of Christ. For all things are possible to him.

(Lecture - Power . . 7 - 23 - 1968)

Persistent Assumption

But you, knowing now what you do know . . you can play this game beautifully, all in love. All you do is follow the Golden Rule: "Do unto others as you would have them do unto you." You can't go wrong! You can't go wrong. If anyone asks you to hear that someone is dead that he may get their estate, that is not what you want done to you, therefore you would not accept that request. "Go elsewhere, but don't come to me." But if they ask you to help them hear that they have a fortune, or that they are secure, or that they are contributing to the world's good, believe them, because I would like to do those things myself. Who wouldn't want to be secure? Who wouldn't want to feel that he contributes to the good of his environment? To the good of his country? Anyone wants to feel that. Therefore, if the request was along that line, believe it when you hear it. So, dare to assume that they have what they now request, and if you persist in that assumption, they will get it. You don't have to concern yourself as to how they are going to get it.

A friend of mine wrote me concerning my book, "Feeling Is The Secret," that we never get what we want, we only get what we are. Well, he knows if he reads the book carefully that you can make what you want what you are, by an assumption. I start with a want. Yes, I want to be. By the mere saying that I want to be, I am confessing that I am not. Well, if I dare to assume that I AM what reason tells me that I am not until that wanting ceases to be, because I feel that I AM it . . before I have the evidence to testify and to bear witness to it, I must precede it by an assumption that I AM it.

When you know what you want, you are told in Scripture, "Believe that you have received it, and you will." That follows your daring mood to believe that you are what, at the moment, reason denies that you are. So, I would not go back on what I have said in that book. I maintain, I've said it correctly; that you do not get what you want, only what you are. Through what you want to be, you can live to be what you are. Assuming it long before there is evidence to support that assumption, then the evidence will come like the fruit coming out of a tree. If you do not know the nature of the tree, wait until the tree is bearing, and when it bears, all arguments vanish, for the fruit will tell you what the tree is. So, all of a sudden, things will happen, based upon what you are.

You don't have to will it. No, people are always trying to will things into being. It is not done willfully, nor even carefully. People gather around themselves everything, and they call themselves "careful operators" . . taking advantage of. No! It is simply the core of integrity. You come right down to: Am I really that? Am I really serious? Well, if I am serious, I should see it all day long as I walk the earth.

(Lecture - Predestined Glory . . Date Unknown)

Persistent Assumption

Jesus is the true identity of every child born of woman. And Jesus-in-you is your own wonderful human imagination. That's Jesus. Now, in this world you can test it. You can test it, because he is the Power of God and the Wisdom of God. How do I test it? I dare to assume that I am what reason denies, and walk in the assumption that I AM that, and if I persist in that assumption, it will harden into fact. And if "by Him all things were made, and without Him was not anything made that was made", and then suddenly I am confronted with the thing itself, having assumed that it is, and I assumed it when reason denied the fact, haven't I found Him? If "by Him all things are made," and I dare to assume what my senses deny and reason denies it, and yet I persist in the assumption, and then eventually it hardens into fact . . well, did I not find the One Who makes things? And if "by Him all things are made, and without Him was not anything made that is made," and I have found exactly how I did it . . and I did it by simply assuming that I AM what I would like to be, even though at the moment of my assumption everything denies that I could possibly be that, and then I became that . . well then, I have found Jesus.

I only assumed that I was what my reason denied. How did I do it? By imagining. I have found my imagination to be the Lord Jesus, but eventually I will awaken as the Lord Jesus. How do I know? I know from experience that everything recorded in Scripture concerning Jesus, I have experienced . . everything, I don't care what it is.

(Lecture - Pre-Existence . . 7 - 16 - 1969)

Persistent Assumption

The ideal we serve and hope to achieve is ready for a new incarnation; but unless we offer it human parentage it is incapable of birth. We must affirm that we are already that which we hope to be and live as though we were, knowing like Dr. Millikan, that our assumption, though false to the outer world, if persisted in, will harden into fact.

The perfect man judges not after appearances; he judges righteously. He sees himself and others as he desires himself and them to be. He hears what he wants to hear. He sees and hears only the good. He knows the truth, and the truth sets him free and leads him to good. The truth shall set all mankind free. This is our spiritual revival. Character is largely the result of the direction and persistence of voluntary attention.

"Think truly, and thy thoughts shall the world's famine feed; Speak truly, and each word of thine shall be a fruitful seed; Live truly, and thy life shall be a great and noble creed."

(Radio Talk - Be What You Wish To Be, Be What You Believe . . 1951)

Persistent Assumption

By imagination, we are all reaping our destinies, whether they be good, bad, or indifferent. Imagination has full power of objective realization and every stage of man's progress or regression is made by the exercise of imagination.

I believe with William Blake,

"What seems to be, is, to those to whom it seems to be, and is productive of the most dreadful consequences to those to whom it seems to be, even of torments, despair, and eternal death."

By imagination and desire we become what we desire to be. Let us affirm to ourselves that we are what we imagine. If we persist in the assumption that we are what we wish to be, we will become transformed into that which we have imagined ourselves to be. We were born by a natural miracle of love and for a brief space of time our needs were all another's care. In that simple truth lies the secret of life.

Except by love, we cannot truly live at all. Our parents in their separate individualities have no power to transmit life. So, back we come to the basic truth that life is the offspring of love. Therefore, no love, no life. Thus, it is rational to say that, "God is Love."

Love is our birthright. Love is the fundamental necessity of our life.

"Do not go seeking for that which you are. Those who go seeking for love only make manifest their own lovelessness and the loveless never find love. Only the loving find love and they never have to seek for it."

(Radio Talk - By Imagination We Become . . 1951)

Persistent Assumption

We are told that whatever we desire, when we believe we already have received it, we will. This promise is based upon the premise that imagining creates reality. There is nothing you cannot become or have as an objective fact, if you believe you already have it. No restriction or condition has been placed upon the power of belief. If you will deny the evidence of your senses, suspend your reason, and persuade yourself that you are now the person you want to be, you will become it! Ask yourself how your friends would see you if you now embodied the idea you desire. Your true friends would rejoice, would they not? Then, if this statement in the Book of Mark is true, all you have to do is persist in believing your assumption is true, and it will harden into fact.

I do not care what the world will tell you, imagination creates its reality. All of these precepts must be accepted literally, for they are literally true. What person truly believes that he was born to be what he is today? He may have been born into a family of great wealth, and . . being surrounded by it . . he takes wealth for granted; but that is an assumption. He may even believe he is entitled to it; but if you checked into his family tree, you would discover that his father or grandfather had a vision which became his reality. And if he who was born into wealth does not know the principle that supports it, he can lose the money and never regain it again. But you who know that everything is based upon an assumption realize that no one can take anything from you that you really want!

Take everything I have, but leave me with the knowledge of how I received it in the first place and I will reproduce it again by the seed of contemplative thought. This is stated so clearly in the 11th chapter of the Book of Mark: "Whatever you desire, believe you have received it and you will." These words are put into the mouth of one called Christ Jesus, who said, "I AM the truth." If Jesus Christ only speaks the truth, will you believe him? Live by his words! Accept on faith that which you do not understand, and apply that which you do. How would you feel if your desire were true? Catch the feeling and sustain it. Persist in your assumption and in a way that no one knows, it will become true for you!

(Lecture - Signs From Above . . 6 - 24 - 1968)

Persistent Assumption

Right now you can use your powerful imagination to assume you are what at the moment your senses and reason deny. Walk in this assumption, knowing you are all imagination, and all things are possible to you. Dare to believe in the reality of your assumption and watch the world play its part relative to its fulfillment. Your assumption may appear to be false when first imagined; but if you will persist, it will harden into fact, because God is he who is doing the assuming. All of the objective facts you see here on earth are only shadows, which fade because imagination is their reality.

(Lecture - Spiritual Sensation . . 5 - 6 - 1969)

Persistent Assumption

If it takes unnumbered tens of thousands to play their part to aid the birth of your imaginal act, they will, not even knowing they are playing the part you assigned them. You don't need to know who they are. All you are required to do is persist in your imaginal act, because that is God in action; but if you quit, then you do not know who God is. You are told: "The word that goes forth from my mouth shall not return unto me void, but must prosper in the thing for which I sent it." That word is an imaginal act. It must return to you and bring you the fruit of that which you intended when you sent it out.

(Lecture - Spiritual Sensation . . 5 - 6 - 1969)

Persistent Assumption

A man who is now poor and embarrassed because of his poverty . . he can still dream, and dream of wealth, dream of security; but it's a shadowy state. It is something that seems to him almost impossible if he is going to use reason. He will say, "How is this thing possible? Because I have no background either intellectually or financially or socially to even hope to achieve that sort of thing." But if he knows who He really is . . the Spirit of God who creates all things dwells in him, and that he can detach that Indwelling Being from the body that he "wears," and actually enter his dream, . . the dream will take on reality. And, if he persists in it, it will objectify itself in this world.

(Lecture - Step Into The Picture
(Who God Really Is) . .5 - 10 - 1971)

Persistent Assumption

So I tell you: don't forget God's law, for "Blessed is the man who delights in the law of the Lord, for in all that he does he prospers."

Now tonight you take it, though everything in the world denies it. Reason denies it, your friends will deny it, and you dare to assume you are the man . . already the man, already the woman . . you would like to be, and that things are already what you would like them to be. And as you dare to assume that you are, and you walk in that assumption just as though it were true, in a way that no one knows you will be led across a series of events toward the fulfillment of that assumption, and no power in the world can stop it if you are persistent in that assumption.

Believe that imagining creates reality. "Therefore I tell you, whatever you ask in prayer, believe that you receive it, and you will." Just as simple as that . . but how to believe that I receive it? If at this very moment I believe that I have received what today I deny, I would look at the world differently. I wouldn't see it prior to that fulfillment. I would now mentally look at the world, and I should see it as I would see it, were it true that I have become the man I want to be. I would commune with my wife, my daughter, my friends, from that assumption, and though no physical thing in the world could force me, I still should persist in the belief it is done, and carry on that assumption, and sleep in the belief that it has taken place just as though it were true. And if I do, may I tell you: I know from experience it will come true on this level. It is already true the very moment I believe it; at that moment is the creative act.

(Lecture - Summary . . 1 - 29 - 1963)

Persistent Assumption

This platform is concerned only with the great secret of life. Here we are convinced that the Supreme Power that created and sustains the universe is Divine Imagining, and it does not differ from human imagination save in degree of intensity. So God-in-man is your wonderful Imagination; that is God. We tell you that Imagination creates Reality, but bear in mind that at this human level on earth it takes time and persistence. If we will persist in the image, live in it, sleep in it, breathe in it, it will crystallize into tangible form. Night after night we take different facets of this truly great secret, and as we turn to the greatest book on Imagination in the world, we treat it differently. So, as we turn to it, bear in mind that the Bible is addressed to the Imagination, not to the man of sense or the man of reason . . the one that is "lost" or "dead" or "sound asleep."

We will take a simple little verse and show you why it is not addressed to the natural man, "That which is, already has been; that which is to be, already has been; and God seeks what has been driven away." The "natural man" cannot grasp that, for to him reality is based only on the evidence of the senses. The man of reason could justify the verse's end, saying if it has any meaning then the writer must mean recurrence. The sun comes every day and the moon completes its cycle and the seasons come and go. If we took a picture of the universe today, the scientists can compute how long it will take to return to this point in the picture. So the intellectual man could justify the verse; but that is not what is meant, for it is addressed not to the man of reason or the man of sense, but to the man of Imagination. What is it all about? "That which is, already has been; that which is to be, already has been, and God seeks what has been driven away."

(Lecture - That Which Has Already Been . . 10 - 6 - 1959)

Persistent Assumption

God is the great dreamer in man, bound in a deadly dream until he forms the image called Christ, in himself. Only when Christ is formed in man will he awaken from his dream of life. Now, on this level you can be bound in a dream, too. Perhaps you would like to be a great artist. That is your dream, your image. How would you feel right now if you were? Can you believe your assumption is true even though your reason and senses deny it? Can you persist in your imagination, as the highest level of your being persists in his image?

We are told: "When you pray, believe you have received it and you will." Prayer is not a lot of empty words, but imagination braced in feeling. Every Sunday people go to church, say the Lord's Prayer, and come out of the building just the same as they were when they went in. Their words were empty, as no prayer was answered. Now they are going to stop praying to their demoted mythological saints, for that is all saints are. The 115th Psalm describes these so-called saints, and tells us that those who believe in them are just as stupid as those who make and sell them.

While here in this world, I asked myself how I would go about being the artist who could make myself into the image of a successful minister of the word of God. I knew I would have to start on the highest level by assuming I had finished what

I was starting to do, and I knew I would have to remain faithful to that end, that image. This I have done.

The most creative thing in us is to believe a thing into objective existence. Can you believe that something is already objective to you, even though your mortal eyes cannot see it? Can you walk, drenched in the feeling that it is an objective fact, until it becomes so? That's how everything is brought into being, for all things exist in the human imagination, who is God himself. Imagination is the divine body called Jesus, the Lord. If you are willing to step out, asking no one if it is right or wrong, and dare to walk in the assumption your image is true, it will come to pass.

(Lecture - The Artist Is God . . 5 - 19 - 1969)

Persistent Assumption

When we say that the supreme power that created the universe is the same power that is resident in man, people question that statement. Possibly everyone here owns a Bible, and when you go to court as a witness . . say you are called to swear that you will tell the truth . . and to swear you put your hand on the Bible, or the Word of God. Then you open the Bible and read: "Whatsoever things you desire, believe that you have them...and you shall receive them. And when you stand praying, forgive, if you have aught against your brother, so that your Father in heaven may even so forgive you." You put your hand on the book of truth and swear to tell the truth, and here is this statement in this very book on which you swear, and you don't believe it. It is true. It is based on the statement: Imagination creates reality, for the Bible is addressed to the real man, Imagination. "For the Eternal body of man is The Imagination; that is God himself." (Blake)

Is there anything you cannot imagine? Yet many cannot believe what the Book says is true. You admit you can imagine it, yet man does not believe that the thing imagined can be true. But I tell you that if you can imagine it and persist, your persistence will win and you will prove the truth of that statement in Mark 11 given above. However, that is on this level of the world. It is called in the Bible "feasting on the bread and fish," or the loaves and fishes. We can bring about all the changes we desire in our world if we imagine we have it and persist in that state, for if I will persist I will win.

(Lecture - The Bread And The Wine . . 9 - 25 - 1959)

Persistent Assumption

Nothing has ever happened to you that you did not set in motion in your imagination. I tell you: you can be anything you want to be, but when you voice your request, your desire must be genuine. You must so want it that you are willing to remain faithful to your change in position. You cannot assume you have your desire for one little moment and then return to your former state, for if you do you are a double-minded man and will not receive anything from the Lord (as told us in the Book of James). If you want to be successful in business, you can. I don't care how many creditors you owe, or what the bank says you have; if you assume success and persist in that assumption you cannot fail. This is the law by which everyone lives.

(Lecture - The Creator . . 10 - 27 - 1969)

Persistent Assumption

Like the seed, you have to be detached from the Father and fall into the ground to be made alive; for unless a seed falls into the ground it remains alone, but if it falls into the ground and dies it brings forth much. The creative power of your human imagination is the seed which falls into your fleshly body (the red earth called Adam). Hearing the word and applying its truth, your seed is made alive and begins to awake, and you realize who you really are.

You are infinite love, but without the power of imagination, love itself is eternal death. Start now to change your world to conform to your acts of love, but you cannot do it without imagination. Begin with self! Change your world and prove God's power is within you. Then you will know what it is to drink the cup which the Father has given you. It was God's infinite love that detached and allowed you to fall, for this separation is a fall and yet a beginning of a new creation. Just as the seed falls from man and a new creation begins, you fell and began a new creation, for God came with you as your human imagination!

Tonight ask yourself: "Who am I? Where am I?" If you do not like your answers, assume you are the person you would like to be, living where you would like to live. Persist in this assumption and . . although denied by your senses and reason . . if you persist your desires will harden into fact. Start now to take God's gift of his creative power and create!

(Lecture - The Cup Of Experience . . 10 - 27 - 1967)

Persistent Assumption

I know scripture is true, because I questioned it. I started questioning the law because I was interested in things. Having no money, I wanted a trip and I got it. Then I began to tell others, as I wanted to see them take the same principle and test it. As they proved it they told others. I invite you to prove the truth on this level, and have faith that the truth is equally true on the higher level of your being. Continue to test the law for things in this world and accept God's promises on faith, based upon what you have proved by the law.

Do you know what you want? I will tell you a simple way to get it. Simply catch the feeling that you have it and sustain that feeling. Persist in acknowledging the joy of fulfillment. In your imagination tell your friends your good news. Hear their congratulations, then allow him who heard your friends and felt your joy of fulfillment, bring it into your world, for he who can do all these things is within you as your own wonderful I AMness, your Imagination, your consciousness. That is God.

Test God, for he will not fail you. Then, when he proves himself in performance, tell a friend, and continue telling others as you exercise this law. And walk knowing all the other I AM statements are yours. Prove this in the world of shadows and you will prove the other in the world of reality.
Your I AMness is the true eternal reality. Living in a world of shadows, as you declare your I AMness you are declaring eternal truth. When you say, "I AM the resurrection," that is eternal truth. "I AM the life" is eternal truth, as well as "I AM the way." All of these bold certainties preceded with the "I AM" are eternal truths.

So, do not listen to anyone who screams at you from their tower of Babel and tells you of another way, for there is no other way. You don't have to give up meat or only eat fish on Friday in order to enter the way, for the way to the cause of all life is within you. Believe in your I AMness for there is no other God.

(Lecture - The First Principle . . 6 - 9 - 1969)

Persistent Assumption

Take your boss or an employee and represent them to yourself as you want them to be, and believe in the reality of the foundation stone, and then you will not make haste to bring it to pass. For Imagination is creating reality, and in a way no one knows it will be brought to pass if you remain faithful to that foundation stone. It makes no difference who you are or what you have. The man who cannot always sign a check to realize a dream is better off, for he is more awake; for he must use the talent God gave him, which is God himself. If I can always put pressure on someone to get what I want, I will never know I am this machine. But if I have to do it all within myself, then I know.

The Story of Jesus Is Persistent Assumption

A story was told me tonight of a man who had lost his wife at the birth of his son, and the child was taken to St. Louis to be brought up by his wife's sister. This man had tried for seven years to get enough ahead to take a trip to St. Louis to see the child. He constantly tried to see himself getting a job with more money so he could make the trip. He was told that by the right use of this law he should only see himself with his child and let the way be left to God. Following this he was given a job that took him from Los Angeles to New Orleans. But that was not near St. Louis. He took the job and persisted in his dream, and in three months he was transferred to the St. Louis run and given a twenty-four hour layover there every week.

(Lecture - The Foundation Stone - Imagination . . 12 - 1 - 1959)

Persistent Assumption

The game of life, like every game, is played within the framework of certain rules, and any violation of those rules carries a penalty. You and I are playing this game from morning to night, and should therefore learn its rules in order to play it well.

Ecclesiastes gives us this rule: "Even in your thought do not curse the king, or in your bed chamber curse the rich, for a bird will carry your voice or some winged creature tell the matter." And Mark gives us another, as: "Whatever you desire, believe that you have received it and you will." If you must believe you have received your desire in order to attain it, then you must start your game by believing it is finished. You must feel yourself into and partaking of your goal. And you must persist in that feeling in order to achieve it.

Now, another rule is said in this manner: "Cast your bread upon the water and you will find it after many days." In other words, do not be concerned as to how it is going to happen . . just do it. This statement hasn't a thing to do with doing good as the world defines the word. Jesus was a carpenter. The word means one who produces from seed . . as a flower, a tree, the earth.

The prophecy of the Old Testament is the seed which a carpenter called Jesus brings to birth. He comes not to abolish the law and the prophets but to fulfill them. The word, 'bread' in the statement: "Cast your bread upon the waters," means to devour; to consume. Water is a euphemism for semen, that living water which carries the sperm of man. The creative act is psychological, not physical; yet the intentions are the same. You must cast your bread upon the waters with passion! You must be consumed with the desire and literally on fire with love for its possession, for an intense imaginal act will always draw unto itself its own affinity.

Winston Churchill departed this world a very successful man; however, during his life he had many failures. Then one day he made this discovery, which changed his life. These are his words: "The mood decides the fortunes of people, rather than the fortunes decide the mood."

Let me put it this way: The game of life is won by those who compare their thoughts and feelings within to what appears on the outside. And the game is lost by those who do not recognize this law. Being consumed by anger, they see no change in their world. But if they would change their mood, their circumstances would change. Then they would recognize the law behind their world.

There are those who are depressed all day long and remain that way all of their life. I remember back in New York City, when I would see certain people walking in my direction I would want to cross the street, because I did not want to hear their depressing stories. They would spend hours telling about their wife or husband, their children or grandchildren, and each story geared to depression. Never changing their mood, their world never changed. Seeing no change, they would not recognize a law between the inner world they maintain and the outer world of response.

But if you apply this law you can predict your future. Feel a new mood rise within you. Sustain it and soon you will meet people who embody this new state. Even inanimate objects are under the sway of these affinities. In a certain mood I have gone to my library and removed a book I have not touched in years. And when I casually open it, I find confirmation of my mood. A table, though remaining the same, will be seen differently based upon your momentary mood, for everything reflects it. It is your mood which decides your fortune, not your fortune that decides your mood. People feeling poor attract poverty, not knowing that if they felt rich they would attract wealth.

In the Book of Proverbs, it is said: "The spirit of man is the lamp of the Lord." Now, the lamp of the Lord is the light of the world. We contain that light; and nature . . the genie . . is our slave, fashioning the world as our mood dictates. By nature I mean all of humanity . . the animal, plant, and mineral world. In fact, everything that appears on the outside is a slave of this lamp. Fashioned from within, this slave will fashion your world to reflect your thoughts; and no power can stop their fulfillment. Become aware of what you are thinking, and you will recognize a law between your mood and your surrounding circumstances. Then you will predict with certainty, because you know certain events . . being in harmony with your mood . . must appear. Everything . . whether a living being or an inanimate object such as a book . . must appear to bear witness to your mood.

Now, in order to play the game of life, you must know what you want to replace what you have. When you know what it is, you must assume the feeling that you have it. Although your reason and senses will deny its existence, persistence will cause your assumption to harden into fact and objectify itself upon your screen of space. Play the game this way. You may think it doesn't work, but that's because you have not tried it. You may believe the idea is stupid, but I tell you: the mood decides your fortune. Believe me, for I have proved this principle over and over again in my life.

(Lecture - The Game Of Life . . 3 - 7 - 1969)

Persistent Assumption

Let us learn the rules of the game of life and play it. Life itself is caused by the assemblage of mental states, which occurring creates that which the assemblage implies. My friend mentally heard the words he would hear if his desire for his friend were fulfilled. Its assemblage, occurring within him, created the event to be played out in the game of life.

After you have assembled your mental state and allowed it to occur within you, you do not have to repeat the act. You cast your bread upon the water the moment you felt relief. Although you do not have a physical expression in a sexual manner, relief is possible; and of all the pleasures of the world, relief is the most keenly felt. When someone you dearly love is late, you anxiously await that key in the door. And when you hear their voice, your relief is keenly felt. That is the same kind of relief you will have when you have imagined correctly.

If you find it necessary to recreate the act every day, you are not casting your bread upon the water. You may imagine over and over again, but you are only going to impregnate once; and if you reach the point of relief, your bread has been cast upon the water to return, perhaps in the matter of an hour. I have had the phone ring . . minutes after I have imagined it . . to hear confirmation that it has happened. Sometimes it has taken days, weeks, or months; but I do not repeat the action once I have done it and felt the feeling of relief, for I know there is nothing more I need to do.

Learn to consciously play this game of life, for you are unconsciously playing it every day. I am sure the millions who are on relief feel the government owes them a living; but there is no government, only we who pay taxes. The government has no money and can only give what it takes from our pockets. Those on relief are complaining, claiming they are not getting enough out of our pockets, and that mood persists throughout their day.

Their mood never varies, so they see no change and recognize no law between the mood they are sustaining and the outer world they dislike. If they were told that their mood was causing the phenomena of their life, they would deny it. No one wants to feel that he is solely responsible for the conditions of his life, yet there is no other cause. God is the only cause and he is man's own wonderful human imagination.

(Lecture - The Game Of Life .. 3 - 7 - 1969)

Persistent Assumption

I urge you to use your imagination lovingly on behalf of everyone, and believe in the reality of your imaginal acts. If you have a friend who would like to be gainfully employed, listen carefully until you hear his voice tell you of his new position. Feel his hand clasp yours. See the smile on his lips. Use every sense you can possibly bring to bear into the imaginal scene. Persist until you feel the thrill of reality, then drop it and let that scene fulfill itself on the outside. We are told that the kingdom of heaven is like a mustard seed. Your imaginal act created for your friend in the kingdom of heaven is that seed. Don't pick it up to see if it is growing; just leave it alone, and it will grow and bloom as a solid fact in your world. Then you will have found this hidden cause within you called Christ.

Christ, the power and wisdom of God, is in you as your own wonderful eternal being. He will never leave you or forsake you as told us in the 13th chapter of Hebrews. If, perchance, one day you are swept into an unlovely state and go through hell, remember: there is that in you who will not leave you or forsake you; and if you know this principle you can detach yourself from the state and it will vanish, as you move into a more desirable one.

There is truly nothing new under the sun. That which was recently recorded in the Atlantic Monthly is the same as that which was recorded in Genesis as the first frightful act, when Cain slew his brother Abel. This same act is taking place over and over again, and if a man knows how to detach himself he need not be pulled into that state. While in the army I was told I could not get out, but I dared to assume I was out. I acted, in my imagination, as I would act were I free to come and go as I chose. I persisted in this assumption for nine days. Then the one who first denied my request granted my freedom, and that day I was honorably discharged.

(Lecture - The Game Of Life . . 3 - 7 - 1969)

Persistent Assumption

I am telling you the secret of God every time I take this platform. I am playing the part of Judas every Monday and Friday night. I play it every time I talk to a friend. If they call me on the phone, I am betraying the secret. "I have come, not to abolish the law and the prophets, but to fulfill them." So, I tell you the Law. I reinterpret the Law psychologically, and tell you that, "An assumption, though false, if persisted in will harden into fact." [Sir Anthony Eden]

Two thousand years ago you heard that same statement told in this manner, "Whatever you desire, believe that you have received it, and you will." It's the identical thing told in a more modern form . . the same thing. If you dare to assume this, that or the other, and persist in your assumption, it will harden into fact and project itself on the screen of space. That is the Law. It's psychological.

(Lecture - The Hidden Secret Of God . . 4 - 12 - 1971)

Persistent Assumption

It is not before Abraham was, I AM, but before Abraham, was I AM! Here we see that the fountainhead of everything is I

The Story of Jesus Is Persistent Assumption

AM! Although the horrors of the world may deny a divine event, remember the story of the tapestry. Scripture calls the unlovely side "below," while the lovely side is called "above." The Risen Christ is made to say: "You are from below and I AM from above. You are of this world and I AM not of this world." In other words, you who have not experienced scripture are from below, while those who have are from above. You are of this world, while they are no longer a part of this world. But, because we are all one, you will be lifted up as the Risen Christ.

Any desire is yours to fulfill if you will not lose confidence in I AM. Attach anything to it and it will grow. If your desire is to be rich, say to yourself: I AM rich . . and think from that assumption. If you want to be known, claim you already are. You can be anything you want to be by the act of assumption. Wear your desire as though it were true now, and your assumption . . though denied by your senses . . when persisted in will harden into fact by objectifying itself and becoming a reality.

But that is not the purpose of life. There is only one purpose, which is to fulfill scripture. And when God makes himself known in you . . an individual . . and you tell your experiences, the world will deny them. But I tell you: you cannot turn to another and say I AM; and you cannot divide it, for I AM is one!

(Lecture - The Incarnate Revelation . . 2 - 20 - 1969)

Persistent Assumption

Your own wonderful human imagination is the cause of the restrictions on the freedom that you enjoy today. There is no other cause but the Lord, who is the Father, who is the potter, and if he is your own wonderful human imagination, to whom can you turn to praise or blame for the circumstances of your life? The blind leaders of the blind blame society or the government for the causes of the phenomena of their life.

But I tell you, there is no other cause; for there is no one outside of self. Society, the government, your family, or friends, are all within you. Although they appear to be pushed out, there is not a thing that does not now exist in you; as Divine Imagination (the Lord God Almighty) has reproduced Himself in you . . the human imagination; and Divine Imagination contains all things within Himself.

Do not look to another as the cause of your misfortune. If you are perceiving a thing, it is penetrating your brain; therefore it exists in you. That which you are perceiving appears to exist in the surrounding world independent of your perception of it, but don't wait for it to change. If you desire a change in that which you are perceiving, you must produce the change in yourself. Ask no one to help you; simply persist in your new thoughts and let your changed thinking reproduce itself in your outside world, for it is only an out-picturing of the world of thought within you. Try it. You can change your world as this prisoner did. In his imagination he moved in time to the day after his escape. You can do the same. Would your friends know of your success the day after it was achieved? Would they get together to discuss it? Make their gathering the scene from which you start. What would they say? Would some of them be jealous? Some happy for you? Put them all together and eavesdrop on their conversation. Then believe in what you have heard. Persist and your success is assured.

(Lecture - The Lord Our Potter . . 11 - 7 - 1969)

Persistent Assumption

Tonight, set your hope fully upon this grace that is coming to you; for Christ in you is your hope of glory! Do you not realize that Jesus Christ is in you? Test yourself and see, for all things are possible to him. Think of something you would like that reason says you cannot have. Now, assume it's yours.

Your assumption, though false in the sense that it is denied by your reasonable mind, if persisted in will harden into fact. You do not need to know the means that will be employed to bring your assumption to pass; all you are required to do is persist in your assumption and allow your own wonderful human imagination to give it to you.

All things are possible to your imagination. It's up to you to provide the necessary link between your assumption and its fulfillment. That link is faith. Having assumed your desire is fulfilled, your faith in that assumption will cause it to harden into fact. That is the law.

Test this law, and if you prove it in performance, it will not matter to you if it seems irrational to others. Tonight, leave this auditorium in the assumption that you are what you would like to be; and if tomorrow your assumption can be seen as fact by the world round about you, then you have found Christ, he who is within you as your hope of glory.

Man is forever coming up with fantastic ideas like going to the moon. At the time, the idea seemed impossible, yet in time man does go to the moon. So you see, nothing is impossible to God .. but nothing!

Simply name that which seems so impossible to you, then assume that you have it. Walk in the assumption it is now an objective fact and see how God works. I tell you, in a way that you do not know, and you could not possibly devise, you will be led across a bridge of incident to the fulfillment of that state. All you have to do is ignore the evidence of your outer senses and go about your own wonderful business assuming the feeling of the wish fulfilled. Your assumption, instead of receding into the past, will advance into the future and you will walk right into its fulfillment.

(Lecture - The Nature Of God .. 9 - 22 - 1969)

Persistent Assumption

Your own wonderful human imagination is the being that I speak of when I speak of God. When I say, "God became as we are, that we may be as He is," I am speaking of your imagination. And you cannot get away from your imagination. "And by Him all things were made, and without Him was not anything made that was made." That's your imagination.

There isn't a thing in this world that you see now and call it a fact that wasn't first only imagined: the building; the clothes you wear; the chairs on which you are seated; this little mike; . . everything was first only imagined, and then executed. Well, if all things were made by Him, and without Him was not anything made that was made, . . good, bad or indifferent, try to find some other maker than your own wonderful human imagination. Try to find it. You may say: "Edison did it" . . in his imagination; "Einstein did it" . . in his imagination. Show me one other instrument other than the human imagination that conceived anything in this world, and that is God. "If all things were made by Him, and without Him was not anything made that was made," then you conclude that He must be the human imagination.

So, I tell you, your own wonderful human imagination is the God of Whom I speak! That is the Being that actually will awaken within you. But, now, to get things in this world, assume that you are. "All things are possible to Him." Assume that you are the man that you want to be . . or the woman that you want to be. And, although at the moment of your assumption your reason and your senses deny it, if you dare to persist in that assumption as though it were true, that assumption . . in a way unknown to your rational, conscious mind . . will harden into fact. It knows how to actually build that series of events necessary to make it so in your world.

If you really want to be what you call "secure", . . say, in finances, dare to assume that you are secure, and live as though you were; sleep as though you were; and then it will happen in your world that will cause you to leave your present environment and move on into the state that you have assumed. If you wait for things to change before you dare to assume, you will wait forever. Circumstances cannot change of themselves. You change them by changing your concept of Self.

To attempt to change the world before you change your own imaginal activity is to struggle against the very nature of things. Now, you say: "Well, I am reaping these things in my world, and I didn't make them." No, . . you have forgotten the blossom time. What you are now reaping is simply the fruit of some forgotten blossom time. You have a very faulty memory. We all have. We can't remember when we set in motion what we are now reaping as a harvest; but everything in our world was once planted as an imaginal act, and it has not a physical cause, . . it has an imaginal cause. Every natural effect in this world has an imaginal cause, and not a natural cause. A natural cause only seems; it is the delusion of a faulty memory, because man cannot remember the blossom time when he actually set it in motion.

If you will try that; then if you came tonight to hear something more practical, then that is the practical side of this teaching. But may I tell you, I consider that what is most profoundly spiritual is most directly practical. For, if you really give all your attention to this pattern, "and set your hope fully on this unveiling of The Christ you," it will be far more profitable than seeking to become rich in the world. If this thing should only unfold within you, then the world is yours. You don't have any desire for the fantastic claims that people make in this world.

(Lecture - The Pattern Man . . Date Unknown)

Persistent Assumption

Tonight some friends are here who haven't heard me speak in a number of years. When they were last with me I was speaking only of the law, as the promise had not fulfilled itself in me. So for their sake let me say: the promise is the law on a higher level, and the law is very simple.

There are infinite number of states. The state of health, the state of sickness, the state of wealth, the state of poverty, the state of being known, the state of being unknown . . all are only states and everyone is always in a state. We all have one state in which we are very comfortable, so we return to it moment after moment. That state constitutes our dwelling place. If it is not a pleasant state, we can always get out of it. How this is done is the secret I will now share with you. All states are mental. You cannot remove yourself from your present state by pulling strings on the outside. You must mentally adjust your thoughts to proceed from the desired state, all within yourself. You fell into your present state either deliberately or unwittingly; and because you are its life, the state became alive and grew like a tree, bearing its fruit which you do not like. Its fruit may be that of poverty, or distress, heartache, or pain.

There are all kinds of unlovely fruit. But you can detach yourself from your unlovely harvest by making an adjustment in your human imagination. Ask yourself what you would like to harvest. When you know what it is, ask yourself how you would feel if your desire was ready to harvest right now. When you know the feeling, try to catch it. In my own case I find it easier to catch the feeling by imagining I am with people I know well and they are seeing me as they would if my desire were now a fact. And when the feeling of reality possesses me, I fall asleep in that assumption. At that moment I have entered a state. Now, I must make that state as natural as I have made my present state. I must consciously return to my new state constantly. I must feel its naturalness, like my own bed at night. At first the new state seems unnatural, like wearing a new suit or

The Story of Jesus Is Persistent Assumption

hat. Although no one knows your suit is new, you are so conscious of it you think everyone is looking at you. You are aware of its fit and its feeling until it becomes comfortable. So it is with your new state. At first you are conscious of its strangeness; but with regular wearing, the new state becomes comfortable, and its naturalness causes you to constantly return to it, thereby making it real.

Now most of us, knowing what we want, construct it in our minds eye, but never occupy it. We never move into the state and remain there. I call this perpetual construction, deferred occupancy. I could dream of owning a lovely home and hope to go there one day; but if I do not occupy it now, in my imagination, I postpone it to another day. I may wish my friend had a better job. I may have imagined him having it; but if I don't occupy that state by believing he is already there, I have merely constructed the state for him but not occupied it. All day long I can wish he or she were different; but if I don't go into the state and view him from it, I don't occupy the state, so he remains in the unlovely state relative to me. This is the world in which we live.

You can't conceive of a thing that is not part of a state, but the life of any state is in the individual who occupies it. Life cannot be given to a state from without, because God's name is "I AM." It is not "You are" or "They are." God's eternal name is I AM! That is the life of the world. If you would make a state alive, you must be in it. If you are in a lovely, gentle, kind state, you are seeing another as lovely, living graciously, and enjoying life to the utmost. Now, to make that state natural, you must see everyone in your world as lovely, kind, and gentle. Others may not see them in that light, but it doesn't really matter what they think. I am quite sure if I took a survey of what people think of me, no two would agree. Some would say I am a deceiver, while others I am the nearest thing to God. I would find a range stretching from the devil to God, all based upon the state in which the person is in when called upon to define me.

You can be what you want to be if you know and apply this principle, but you are the operant power. It does not operate itself. You may know the law from A to Z, but knowing is not

The Story of Jesus Is Persistent Assumption

enough. Knowledge must be acted upon. "I AM" is the operant power in you. Put your awareness in the center of your desire. Persist, and your desire will be objectified. Learn to use the law, because there is a long interval between the law and the promise. Those who heard me prior to 1959 are unfamiliar with my experiences since that time, and my words may seem strange to you. I cannot deny the law, for I came not to destroy the law and the prophets, but to fulfill them. This I have done.

I have told you that in the resurrection, Man is above the organization of sex, and that Man can change his sex at will. This week I received a letter telling of a vision which testifies to the truth of this statement. This gentleman is married to a lovely girl and is every bit a man, yet this is his experience. He said, "I found myself lying on a bed feeling as though I am a woman. Desiring a man of oriental descent and olive skin, I assumed I had found him. Instantly he appeared and, although no act was performed, I felt the thrill of imagining and instant fulfillment of my imaginal act. Then I awoke." This man's vision verifies what I have been telling you: that in the resurrection Man changes his sexual garments at will, and being above the organization of sex, he does not need the divine image of male/female to create. I think his vision is marvelous. When he returned to this world, he was surprised at the experience; but I say to all: you are destined to know you are every being in the world, bar none!

Like the lady who is so feminine, responding when a shepherd boy called her "father". Although she would not answer my call, she knew I would always find her. I always will, for I . . the Word of God . . was sent as the son of God, and I shall not return to my father void. I must bring back that purpose for which he sent me. I stirred the feeling of the fatherhood of God in her, and I will take back with me those that my father gave me.

But while you are in this world of Caesar, it is important that you master the law. Think of everyone as representing a state. There is no such thing as a good man or a bad man, only good or bad states as you conceive them to be; but the occupant of every state is God. Blake said in his "Vision Of

The Last Judgment: "On this it will be seen that I do not consider either the just or the wicked to be in a supreme state, but to everyone of them states of the sleep which the soul may fail into in its deadly dreams of good and evil when it leaves Paradise following the serpent." Identify yourself with a state and you are pronounced by others to be either good or evil; but you are only in a state. Tonight if you are unemployed, or find it difficult to get a promotion in your present employment, remember: the solution to your present state is still a state!

I hope I have made it clear how to move into states. It is done through the act of assumption with feeling and persistence. Assume health. Stand in its center and clothe yourself with its feeling. Persist in claiming a healthy body and a healthy mind, and your assumption will harden into fact as you move into and objectify the state of health.

(Lecture - The Perfect Image . . 4 - 11 - 1969)

Persistent Assumption

Now, how do I look into the law . . the perfect law which sets me free, the Law of Liberty? I look into my mind. I am now imprisoned. I have heard the sentence. I know exactly how long I'm supposed to serve. Now I look into the Law of Liberty in my mind, and I assume that I AM free . . I AM set free. How? I am not concerned. Who brought it about? I am not concerned. I simply look into the Perfect Law, the Law of Liberty, and I dare to assume that I AM free.

If I dare to assume that I AM free, I rearrange the structure of my mind . . the same mind that heard the sentence that I accepted when I heard it. Now I do not accept it. I look into the perfect law, the Law or Liberty; and if, as I am told in Scripture, I persevere, then I will actually receive that which I am doing. I must not forget what I have done and sleep this night as though I AM in prison. For if I AM now set free, where would I sleep? Let me know, . . exactly where would I sleep? Well, dare to assume that I am sleeping there now. If I sleep in the assumption that I AM free, I am not in jail; even though the bars are there, I don't see them. I close my eyes against them. As Blake tells us "Man's perceptions are not bounded by organs of perception! he perceives more than sense (tho' ever so acute) can discover. And so Reason, or the ratio of all we have already known, is not the same that it shall be when we know more." [from "There Is No Natural Religion."]

If I take this tonight and test it, and it proves itself in the testing, then I have added to my knowledge; and so I know more than before I tested it. So, when I find myself up against something that seems beyond solution, I have found something that can solve it. All I have to do is to rearrange the structure of my mind.

So, I dare to assume that I am the man that I would be, and sleep as though I AM. That is the rearrangement of that structure of the mind. I am the same being; I am Neville. I know exactly those that I knew before, but now I know them differently. I know them, now, as a freed man. But I must not be a hearer of what I heard in Scripture; I must be a doer. I must do it!

So, "Be not a hearer only," Be a doer in the full sense of the word so that actually I do it and persist, . . the word is "persevere" in Scripture.

(Lecture - The Perfect Law of Liberty . . 4 - 2- 1971)

Persistent Assumption

"If the double-minded man comes, who is unstable in all his ways, let him not think he will receive anything from the Lord."

What can you give a man who doesn't know what he wants? I've gone into a restaurant just to prove this principle, sat down, said to the waiter, "What would you like for a tip?" and he is embarrassed.

I said to my friend, "I'll give him what he wants within reason. I'm not going to give him any hundred-dollar bill, but I will give him, if he says a $5 bill," I didn't order that which warranted a $5 bill, and he was embarrassed and embarrassed and embarrassed. All he expected was exactly what he got. He just didn't know. He just had no concept of putting something . . of course, he didn't know it; so how could he put it to the test?

So, I am telling you, you rearrange the structure of your mind. That is all you do. It doesn't differ from Einstein's mind. There is only one Mind. There is only one God. There is only one Lord. Listen to it;

"One body, one spirit, one hope, one lord, one faith, one baptism, one God and Father of us all, Who is above all, through all, and in all."

If He is in you, that's the same One with the one body, the one spirit; so I am not using a different mind. It's the same mind, but differently arranged.

Go into one room, and you see that someone doesn't know what to do with their furniture. Bring someone in who knows how to set a room, come back an hour later after she is through with it, and you will think you are in an entirely different home. My wife used to "pull" that on me all the time! I'd come home and think I had stepped into an entirely strange apartment and wonder if I'm really at home. She was hiding some other place. She had completely rearranged the structure of the furniture. It looked like an entirely different home. But she has that sense, how to do it, and so she did it.

So, with what you have, . . all you need is exactly what you have, for you have the Mind of God! It's not a different mind . . the same mind. And you simply rearrange the mind by a mere assumption. What would the feeling be like, were it true that I am now the man I want to be, now the woman that I

The Story of Jesus Is Persistent Assumption

want to be? And it is added: "but persevere." You must persevere in it.

If I call you now and you answer, that's one thing. Would you respond an hour later to the same call? If you persevere, you will. If now, an hour later, you think of yourself as you now . . when you dare to assume that you are now the man that you want to be; an hour later, are you still assuming that state? If you're not, you are not persevering. You are "the hearer who looked into the mirror, whose natural face" . . he saw it; "then he went his way, and at once forgot what he looked like."

So, if one hour from now you are not still assuming that you are the. man that you want to be, you have forgotten. You are the hearer and not the doer. And he warns us of the vast difference between being a hearer and being a doer. The doer acts.

"God only acts and is in existing beings or man." [Blake, from "The Marriage of Heaven and Hell"]

So, bear in mind that your wonderful world is not bounded by your senses. You perceive far, far more than your senses, no matter how acute they are, could discover. Your senses can't discover what now you are capable of assuming that you are. Your senses dictate what reason will allow; and your reason and your senses are bound together. Go beyond it for what you now know from experience. What you know from the past will not be what you will know when you know more than you now know. Having' done it, and proved it, I know more than I did when I was bounded by my senses.

When I couldn't get out of a certain island on time to meet a commitment in Milwaukee, I knew what I did in the Army. I simply applied the identical thing, and I got out. There was a long, long waiting list . . thousands waiting from all the islands, and only two little ships . . not big ships, two little ships, one carrying not more than 60-odd passengers, one carrying 120, and thousand waiting, and they only came once a month into the island. One every 32 days, and one

The Story of Jesus Is Persistent Assumption

every three and a half weeks. How long would it take to get them all out?

I didn't ask anyone a favor. I didn't ask my brother, who was a powerful businessman in that island. He criticized me for not arranging passage back to America when I left America. He said, "That's the place where you should have done it. That's the power house of the world . . New York City, where all these things are done. And you dared to leave Mew York City when you could have arranged a round trip, and you came here on a one-way ticket?"

Well, I didn't ask any favors of him or any favors of any member of the family. I simply did exactly what I did in the Army* and in 2k hours I was called by the Alcoa Company and given my passage, over thousands who were waiting. It isn't my concern why she did it, or why someone else didn't get it in preference to me when my name was down at the very bottom. I wasn't at the top; I was at the bottom of the list. It isn't my concern. I looked into the perfect law, the Law of Liberty, and I persevered.

I sat in a chair in my hotel room, and there I sat in the chair and assumed I am next to the boat. I am climbing up the gangplank. That's before we had a deep-water harbor; so we had to go out to sea about maybe a half-mile or a mile out to sea on a little tender, and then take the gangplank and go up to the ship. I felt myself bobbing, as you would, on the ocean, and then moving up the gangplank. I smelled the rawness of the sea; got up to the top, . . my mind wandered. I brought it back again and did it all over again. If it wandered again, I brought it back again. I kept on doing it over and over until finally I did it, and fell sound asleep sitting in the chair in the act of doing it. The next day Alcoa calls me and gives me my passage for my wife and my little girl and myself.

So, I am telling you from experience, it doesn't fail; but we must not simply "be hearers of the word; we must be doers of the word, for if you are a hearer and not a doer, you deceive yourself," he tells you, for we are the operant power. This Law doesn't operate itself. It doesn't care if you are good, bad or indifferent.

The Story of Jesus Is Persistent Assumption

Look around the world. Who would think that tonight someone serving a life sentence in our "jail, . . it's the same Mind that sits in the White House; who would think that the one who sits now in the Vatican, . . that mind of the Pope is the same Mind as the one who is groveling on his belly trying to kiss his hand? . . So, on Sunday, . . it will be Palm Sunday, and they do all these things on Palm Sunday, . . the holy palms; and then comes Good Friday; then comes Sunday, and all this will go on and have all the show . . a real show. He who is now being borne on the backs of strong, strapping men does not differ from those who are his servants bearing him . . the same Mind; but they have rearranged their mind to be servants, and he has arranged his mind to be the Father, to be Pope, the great Pope. It's the same Mind!

There is only one Mind in the world. There aren't two minds. That's why I can tell you I know that when He stands before you, He will know you as His Father, and you will know Him as your Son. And because I know Him as my Son, are we not one Mind? Are we not one Being, when the same Being who called me "Father" will one day call you "Father"? Are we not the same Father, the same Mind, the same Spirit, the same body, . . without loss of identity?

So, when you go home tonight, try it. Try it every moment of time. You know tonight what you want to be? I don't care what you want to be. It's simply a rearrangement of the mind; and you rearrange the mind, not through any study or any effort. It's simply a mere assumption. What do I want to be?' Get it clear in my mind's eye. Well then, assume that I AM it.

Listen to the words in the Book of Joel: "Let the weak man say, I AM strong." "Let the weak man say, I AM strong." That's in the Book of Joel. Jehovah God, . . that's what the word would mean . . "Joel."

You are called upon, when you are down, to assume that you are exactly what you want to be; not down, because you don't want to be that. You want to be as free as the wind. Well, assume that you are. And may I tell you? in a way that

The Story of Jesus Is Persistent Assumption

no one knows, you'll become it, but you must persevere. And the word "perseverance" is true. If I don*t believe it, well then one second later I've turned back to my former state and become once more Lot's wife, the pillar of salt. "Salt" is a preservative.

In the old days, the only way to preserve something was to salt it. Not so long ago, when I was a little boy, we caught fish . . an enormous quantity of fish, because we didn't have these enormous fleets catching our fish. We had "fish to bum," . . literally bum. If they didn't get in before, say, 3:00 o'clock in the afternoon, what did they have,? They could either put it in the dungheap and make dung out of it, or clean it up and salt it. So they cleaned it up and salted it. It would Keep indefinitely, for we had no refrigeration. So, you salted the fish. Now, we could have salt flying fish, if you wanted it that day; but fish that were not consumed by sundown was discarded, use it for bait the next day or-use-it in the dungheap and fertilize the fields with it.

So, salt is a preservative. So when Lot's wife was turned to salt, she turned back, and went back to her former state; and that is all that it means. She looked back and became a pillar of salt. You turn back to the state that you said you would leave behind you; and looking back, you were salted, you were preserved in it. So, if you turn away to what you really want to be» turn back, you are going to be "salted" in it.

So, I ask you to leave what you are, unless you like what you are. Just portions of what you are today that you like . . all right, wonderful.

There are other portions that you do not like. Well, you don't have to give up everything in your living room when you rearrange the structure of it. There are certain pieces that you will keep. You say change its location, but you will keep it. The same is true with the structure of the mind: you keep certain things, and you let other things go.

Take friends in your world who are not doing well, and rearrange them in your mind's eye. Where they are doing

The Story of Jesus Is Persistent Assumption

well, put that part of the structure in your mind's eye. Rearrange the entire structure, and dare to assume that it's true, and walk in that assumption; and that assumption, though at the moment it is denied by reason and denied by your senses, if you persevere in it, it will harden into fact. This is the Law of Scripture.

He said, "I came not to abolish, but to fulfill the Jewish law and the Jewish prophets." For there was no other Scripture in the First Century but the Jewish scriptures. So, the word "Jew" is not placed before it to qualify it, but it was the only scripture that he knew. He came to fulfill the Jewish law. He reinterpreted the law psychologically, and showed them exactly how it's done.

So, go out, and do not abolish anything. Simply fulfill it. Fulfill the Law, and fulfill the Prophets. The Prophets, when they are fulfilled, that is done by sheer Grace. That comes by Promise, and no one's going to stop it, may I tell you. But you can go on living in a state that you do not wish in this world* but in spite of that, you will still receive the Promise, because it isn't given to the one who is rich and denied the one who is poor. But why remain poor and bat your head off morning, noon and night against the inevitable blows in this world?

I hope you do not wish money for the sake of money; but if you need money, then apply this Law. What would the feeling be like if it were true that I was now free of this pressure . . free of it? Dare to assume that you are, and then persist in that assumption; and that assumption will harden into reality. So, this is my lesson tonight. I think you have found it a very practical one, but I must remind you, you can either be the hearer of what you've heard tonight and not the doer. It is my hope that you will be the doer of what you've heard tonight, so that when you leave here, you leave here in the assumption . . not wait until you get home; leave here in the assumption that you are already the man . . the woman . . that you want to be. And then, between here and home, think of the man that you have assumed that you are, and let that assumption spring in your mind constantly. You are that man! Go to bed in that assumption.

Maybe this night, as it did with me in the Army, something will come, and a voice will speak.

"When vision breaks forth into speech, the presence of Deity is assured"; and maybe you will have confirmation that what you have dared to assume is. I know in my case it came that way. But it will come whether it breaks forth into speech or not, if you persist in the assumption.

(Lecture - The Perfect Law of Liberty . . 4 - 2- 1971)

Persistent Assumption

If I don't like the outer world, and I really believe it is caused by the structure of the inner or second man, I then must change his likeness, change his form, by observing how I react to all the unlovely, and how I am not interested in the praise of another, and then begin to feed my sheep, begin to change my thoughts, my feelings, my moods concerning others, and as I begin to change my reactions to people, I find I am changing the structure of the Son of God. And then I automatically produce corresponding changes in my outer world.

If you really like it, and you are bold enough to take it, I promise you a world that is undreamed of by our wise men for even sleep will no longer be the unconscious that it is to the majority of people in the world; that sleep becomes only a doorway into the world where this real you . . the second man . . really lives and moves and has its being. It is a dimensionally larger world, and you enter it quickly in meditation, or night after night in sleep, and you will find opportunities that would dwarf the wildest dream of men here.

So I ask you to really believe it, and try in the short interval of four weeks while we are here to so prove it that you can tell me of the things that have happened to you by putting into practice this Power of Awareness. Learn to become aware at any moment of time of your fulfilled desire. Assume the feeling of your wish fulfilled and learn to become intensely aware of the state fulfilled, that you may look upon your world and describe it relative to your fulfilled desire. And learn then to sustain that mood. You will find in time through the habitual motion of your inner you, after a little while, because it always travels according to habit, it will move through habit into the feeling of the wish fulfilled, and the moment it is a natural wearing to itself, it starts to change the outer world to reflect the inner change of your mind.

Now, I hope you will take it, but there is no power in the world that can compel you to take it. You are as free as the wind to take it or not to take it. If you would rather persist in the belief that your Savior lived years ago and died for you and through his death, external to yourself, you are saved; you are entitled to believe it.

As I told you earlier, because the inner you is molded in harmony with the sum total of all your beliefs, you will continue to have visible proof of the truth of that belief. For you will find millions believing with you, and you will believe that the numbers make it right, and so you will contribute to the whole vast traditions of men. If you want to come out and be apart and find your savior where you will only find Him, within yourself, by setting your imagination to observe itself, you must come to the same conclusion . . that this ultimate reality that men call God, that the Ancients defined as I AM, is your own wonderful consciousness and that IT in action, or the Son, or Christ Jesus, is your imagination. And then, having discovered, you start really to feed the sheep and you will stop, as of now, this walking of your Savior in the mud.

Now I see my time is up, and so at this moment I'll take the chair and let us all join in exercising our imagination lovingly on behalf of another. Simply imagine that they are talking to you, and they are telling you what they wish they could tell you, and you listen as though you heard, and then you will put into practice that first verse of the fifth chapter of the Book of Ephesians: "Be ye imitators of God as dear children" . . for how would I imitate my Father? "He calls things that are not now seen as though they were, and the unseen becomes seen". That is the way my Father called things into being, and I am called upon to be an imitator of my Father as a dear child. For now I will call the imaginary voice. I will listen as though I heard what I want to hear. I will look as though I am seeing what I want to see, and if I persist in my listening and my looking, I will then be imitating my Father as a dear child, and he will not fool me. He will call into flesh, into objective reality, that which I have assumed that I have heard and I have seen.

(Lecture - The Power Of Awareness . . 1953)

Persistent Assumption

You are told in scripture, if two different persons agree in testimony it is conclusive. If I want to be healthy I am confessing I am not, so we are in conflict. We must now agree to be one. Assuming health, I hear my relatives and friends tell me they have never seen me looking better. Now the state called health, and I who didn't feel well, have agreed in testimony. This is true for any state. If I am impoverished and would like to be secure, there is conflict. Assuming wealth I resolve the conflict, for the two states have agreed in testimony, and as I persist it is conclusive. When you enter a state say, "Let there be light." Let it become luminous so you can see it, that you may manifest it in your world, and it will be so.

(Lecture - The Primal Wish . . 10 - 24 - 1966)

Persistent Assumption

You can't get away from your own imagination. You can't get away from it because that's your own being. That is the reality. But it suffers with you. He is the Lord Jesus Christ within you. Now test Him tonight. Test Him for the good. Do you want a better job when they say they are letting people out? Forget what the papers say. Forget what anything says. "All things are possible to the Lord Jesus Christ."

If you don't have enough money, forget what the paper says, you assume that you have it. "All things are possible to God." He sets no limits whatsoever on the power of believing. Can you believe it? Well try to believe it. Try to believe, first of all, in God. Well God is your own imagination. Well believe in Him; that whatever you can imagine is possible.

Can you imagine that you have now the kind of a job that you want? The income that would come from it? The fun in the doing of the work? Well then walk as though it were true; and to the best of your ability believe that it's true. And that assumption though denied by your senses, . . though the world would say it is false; if you persist in it, it will harden into fact. This is the law of your own wonderful imaging. Believe it, and it will become a reality.

(Lecture - The Secret Of Imagining . . Date Unknown)

Persistent Assumption

Can you imagine what it would be like if you were the man (the woman) you would like to be? Sustain that imaginal act as though it were true, and no power in the world can stop it from becoming true, because there is no other power. Try it beginning tonight. Take a glorious concept of life. Nothing less than the very best, and simply imagine it to be true about you and those you love. Start with your immediate circle and . . although at the moment your circle may deny it by reason of what they are doing . . persist in your assumption as though it were true, and it will harden into fact.

Grant all of your sleeping brothers their right to pursue God in some other direction. They will never find him in any other way, save by experiencing the story of Jesus Christ. Then and only then will they know the true knowledge of God.

(Lecture - The Secret Of Imagining . . Date Unknown)

Persistent Assumption

One night a lady decided to test me by embracing a huge bouquet of roses. She caught the aroma of the rose and completely saturated herself with it, then she dropped the thought. This lady lived in the Waldorf Towers, and when she returned to her room the following evening she discovered three dozen roses had been placed there. It appeared that the Queen Mother was in New York City and had attended a banquet in her honor. Special roses were grown and [brought] there for her pleasure. The next day the maitre d' sent three dozen roses to this lady's room. She put her sense of smell to the test and within 24 hours her room was filled with roses.

I don't care who you are, I invite you to take the challenge. In the 13th chapter of 2 Corinthians you are asked this question: "Test yourself and see. Do you not realize that Jesus Christ is in you? Unless of course you fail to meet the test." Test God's power and God's wisdom, for encased in love you are testing the Christ seed within you. You can take anything and test this power. Do it just for the fun of it. Hold a long-stemmed rose in your hand. Touch its velvety petals and smell its heavenly aroma. Make a pledge to yourself that you will live by your imagination, for God has promised that you can assume a state and it will become a fact in his words: "Whatever you desire, believe you have received it and you will." It can't be stated any clearer than that. These are the words of an awakened man who is God, for every man who awakes in Jesus Christ is God, He who is forever extending himself.

So when you know what you want, construct a scene which would imply that you have it. Enter the scene by touching the articles there, listening to the sounds that may be heard, seeing with your spiritual eye, and smelling its odor with your spiritual nose. Bring all of your senses to bear upon the scene implying the fulfillment of your dream. After you have done it persist in the awareness that your desire is already a fact, for the present moment does not recede into the past, but advances into the future to confront you. You will walk into your future and confront the fulfillment of your desire, which began as a dream.

You may think your yesterdays are in the past, but God knows you will meet them in the future, for your future is always confronting you and bringing in the harvest of what you are doing now.

(Lecture - The Ultimate Sense . . 6 - 20 - 1969)

Persistent Assumption

There is no other God, other than he who is housed within you. When you say, "I AM" you are speaking God's name, the God I ask you to trust . . for there is no other. We are told to "Make no graven image unto me." If you make an image out of marble or metal in the shape of another and worship it, you have created a false God.

A friend recently shared a wonderful experience with me. It seems a neighbor was forever dropping in on her, constantly telling horrible stories about her friends. She tried to tell the woman how to change things by using her imagination, but she would not listen. And although she imagined her as a fine, positive, happy person, she remained in her negative state.

Realizing the lady was a character my friend had to overcome, she began to change her thoughts. In her imagination she told the neighbor that she loved her. This she persisted in doing, until one day she realized she really did. That night she had this dream.

She found herself sitting in the shade of a beautiful tree. A figure approached, looking like a goddess, in a long white gown with loose sleeves and a silver belt. Suddenly she realized it was her friend, who came to say goodbye. They embraced and she felt a surge of love for that woman like she had never known for anyone before.

The next day this lady came to her door and said: "I gave my notice this morning and have come to say goodbye." Then my friend added this thought: "If I could fall as much in love with the being within me as I did with this lady, I would be completely transformed . . which in turn, would produce great changes in my outer world of effects, for now I know my friend's transformation took place within me."

Scripture tells us to love God because he first loved us, and that we should imitate him as a dear child. How is this done? By falling in love! Whether your desire be for wealth, fame, health, or marriage, you must fall in love with the state. My friend fell in love, and so transformed the lady she will never again encounter that state.

God uses man to express love and hate, for man is the agent to express the qualities of I AM. There is no other God! You will find other characteristics of God, but those who know his name put their trust in I AM!

Put your trust in God's name. Knowing what you want, believe that your assumption will make it a fact. Believe that you need no one on the outside to aid you, for all things are possible to God. Assume things are as you want them to be, for an assumption, persisted in will harden into fact!

(Lecture - Trust In God . . 10 - 13 - 1967)

Persistent Assumption

Paul tells us that no matter what he has done or did not do, he puts it behind him and stretches forward towards what lies ahead. Paul's ideal was to be called to the highest point of God. I hope this is your ideal, too, but perhaps it is not. Maybe other things are pressing upon you, such as the need for money. If so, make that your objective, but use the same technique.

Put the past behind you. Do not look back and become like Lot's wife who turned into a pillar of salt . . which is a preservative. You always put what you want to preserve in brine. If you turn back and dwell upon the state you want to leave behind, you have placed it in brine and will become it once more. But if you will turn your back upon the past regardless of what you have or have not done, and stretch forward to what you want to be or do and remain faithful to your desire . . nothing can stop you from achieving it. You will become the man you assume you are, if you persist in the assumption that you are already there!

(Lecture - Walk By Faith . . 11 - 6 - 1967)

Persistent Assumption

The treasures of earth can be withdrawn at any moment, but the treasures in the instructions I am giving you now are forever. Only one being was pierced, and that is Jesus Christ, your true identity. The crucifixion is over. You have been crucified with Christ, and your resurrection will take place in you, in its own wonderful time.

I ask you to test your imagination! Go all out and believe in what you have imagined. Do not try to influence anyone. Instead, put all of your energies into clarity of form.

If a certain desk designates that you are occupying a desired position, occupy that desk. Enter into the image, and you will realize your vision. Sit in the chair behind that desk and view the room. Persist in thinking from that point of view. If you do not physically occupy that chair tomorrow, and begin to doubt, ask yourself: "What am I doing, remembering and not imagining?" Then return to your chair behind that desk!

(Lecture - What Are You Doing . . 10 - 30 - 1967)

Persistent Assumption

Let us take, for those who are here for the first time, truth on this level. A true judgment on this level must conform to the external facts to which it relates. If I should say now, "Isn't it a beautiful dog?" and you look, and there is no dog, my statement is a lie, for there is no dog to support my statement. That's a lie. But the Bible tells us that you can make the statement as I have just made it, and even though at the moment that you make it the senses deny it, you can assume that it is there, and persist in the assumption that it is, and in a way that no one knows, the dog will come there.
You can assume, "I AM rich," and not have a nickel in the bank; in fact, you don't have a bank account. You can assume, "I AM rich, and feel what it would be like if it were true. Now that assumption is a false statement if, at the moment of the assumption, your senses deny it and your reason denies it. So, that is false. Your Bible teaches that it is true if you persist in the assumption; that the assumption, though false, if persisted in, will harden into fact. This is based upon the simple, simple statement that "Imagining creates reality;" that the true being called Jesus Christ is the human imagination. And all things are possible to Christ.

Well, can I imagine it? Yes. Can I believe it to be true? Well, try it. Can I persuade myself that the thing assumed is true? Well, assume it, and assume the feeling of the wish fulfilled. And my assumption, though at the moment of the assumption it is denied by my senses . . denied by my reason; if I persist in my assumption, it will harden into fact. That, I know from my own experience; that, I know from the experiences of hundreds of people who have written to me, and it has worked in their cases.

The Story of Jesus Is Persistent Assumption

If you say, "No," all right, say "No." Continue in your misery. And may I tell you, no one cares. People think that people care? They really don't care! Do you know one person in this world who would rejoice at one's good fortune? And few people even know the meaning of empathy. If another person says to you, "I empathize with you," would you understand it? Do you know, not one person in a thousand or a hundred thousand would understand what he meant? They would think he is sympathizing.

There are many words for sympathy. Let something happen in a block in some neighborhood that is sad. News just came of a horrible thing in the household of one person. The whole neighborhood rushes in to sympathize and commiserate. All sympathize. But let some good fortune befall that house, and they all will say, "Why didn't it happen to me?" They don't say, "Why didn't it . . the misfortune . . happen to me?" "Why didn't the good fortune happen to me?" They don't go to empathize at all.

So, there's only the one word to express the emotion of empathy. It is to rejoice with others who have good fortune with which one could rejoice, but there are many words to sympathize. Well, that's the whole vast world in which we live. So, don't think for one moment that when you go in the back yard to eat worms others are going to join you. All right, eat your worms. They aren't going to join you.

So, if you feel now, "I will not accept this. I will not go against my Lord Jesus Christ. I want to get on my knees and pray to him every day, and pray to him as the intercessor between myself and His Father." May I tell you, you will pray in vain. In vain! There is only one way, and He is housed within you. And that Being is your own wonderful human imagination.

God became as you are, that you may be as He is.

(Lecture - What Is Truth . . 7 - 14 - 1970)

Persistent Assumption

So, don't try to take from another what you feel that no one should do to you. No, the Golden Rule will guide you. You do not take from anyone. You simply promote yourself, and if you are guided by the Golden Rule, doing unto others what you would like them to do to you, you cannot go wrong. So, do not concern yourself with anything on the outside. Just know what you want.

You want to be promoted; you want more income . . well, assume that you have it. To prove that you do have it . . all in imagination, you look at your world and let the world see you as it would have to see you if it were true. You talk with your friends in your imagination as though it is true. You don't tell them anything about it. You do it all in your imagination, and you sleep in that assumption just as though it were true, and then see how it works, I tell you from experience that, without any conscious effort on your part, some series of events will appear, and you will walk across this series of events that will lead you to the fulfillment of your assumption.

So, I know from experience that the assumption, though false, if persisted in will harden into fact. I just simply assume that it is, and having assumed it, the Being in me . . I've found Him; He is Christ . . well, all things are possible to Christ. If Christ is something other than the One of Whom I speak, it's an entirely different matter. But I am convinced that the Christ of Scripture is the human imagination. And having convinced myself that He is, I will believe implicitly in His power. As we are told in Scripture, "Christ is the power of God and the wisdom of God." Well, if He is the power of God and He is the wisdom of God, and He is my imagination . . well, I do not need anyone else! For that is the Creative Power of God. So, what do I need of anyone? I do not need their help if I can imagine.

So, can I dare to assume that I am the one that I would like to be? Can I dare to assume that a friend of mine is as I

The Story of Jesus Is Persistent Assumption

would like him to be, and persuade myself that it is true? Well, then, I do not look for confirmation; I simply assume that it is, and then let it happen, for that thing "has its own appointed hours it will flower. If it seems [to me] long, well, I must wait, for it is sure, and it will not be late." Not for itself. That seed that I just planted may ripen tomorrow; it could be next week, or it may take a year . . I do not know. But I am confident that it must come into being if what I am talking about is true. Simply believe it! Then let it come to pass.

If you do it, you will find no opposition in the world. You do not need the help of anyone in the world . . none whatsoever. All you need is complete faith in God, and God is your own wonderful human imagination. So, faith in your own wonderful imagination is faith in God! For, if God is in me, I should really make every effort to find Him just where He is; and having found Him as the One Who creates all the things in my world . . as I am told in Scripture, "By Him were all things made, and without Him was not anything made that is made."

Well, I look at my world and I try to remember if I ever imagined that. Sometimes I remember vividly that I once imagined that. Well, then, if "all things were made by Him," and I catch it even once . . but if I catch it, say, a dozen times, and I can relate the things that I am now about to harvest to something I once only imagined, then I have found Him, for I have found the secret.

Man has a very poor memory, and he can't quite remember when he set in motion that imaginal act, but he is doing it morning, noon and night. All day long he's imagining, but he forgets what he is imagining, and when it comes up for harvest, he denies his own harvest. But if I can sit down and deliberately write it out if I must, and say I'll do this, I'll do that, I'll do the other, and then in my imagination I do it and give it the tones of reality, and having done it, I simply wait for the result. I go on about my Father's business imagining more lovely things and still more lovely things, and then when it comes up, I know all things must be after their kind. That is the law of life. All things bring forth after their kind. So, it can't be something that I have planted and something different comes up. So, if I plant security by assuming that I am secure . . that is a relative term, I grant you . . to me, what I consider being secure, in time it comes.

(Lecture - Where Are You Staying . . Date Unknown)

Persistent Assumption

Paul found Christ to be his human imagination and urged everyone to test himself. Like Paul, I urge you to test your human imagination. You do not need the money or the time to go anywhere in your imagination, yet you can put yourself there, just as though you had made the trip. If you do, and your circumstances change so that the money and the time appears, allowing you to go, have you not found Jesus Christ to be your imagination? This is what scripture teaches, but man has personified the story and made Jesus Christ into a little idol to bow before, when the true God is the human imagination. All things are made by the human imagination. Imagine something that is not now a fact. Persist in your imaginal act, and when it becomes a fact, you have found God. And once you have found him, never let him go!

At the end of the drama it is said that one who knew Jesus betrayed him. Now, in order to betray someone, you must know his secret! So the one who knows the secret betrays him. That one is self! God is self-revealed. Unless God reveals himself to you, how will you ever know him? Turning to those who did not know him, Jesus said: "Now that you have found me, do not let me go, but let all these go." Let every belief of a power on the outside go, but do not let the belief in your powerful imagination go . . for truth is within you. When you find the Maker in yourself, then no matter what arguments the priesthoods may give, do not believe them, for the Christ you seek is the human imagination.

(Lecture - Your Maker - 1 - 7 - 1969)

Complete Lecture

There Is No Fiction . . 06-07-1968

Fiction is defined as an imaginary construction which is unreal . . as opposed to truth, or reality. But what is real and what is imaginary when, in a spiritual sense, all existing things are imaginary? Mark tells the parable of the fig tree, which . . having been cursed . . was found withered to its roots. Calling attention to this fact, awakened imagination said: "Have faith in God. Truly I say to you, whoever says to this mountain, 'Be taken up and cast into the sea,' and does not doubt in his heart that what he has said will come to pass, it will be done for him. Therefore I tell you, whatever you desire, when you pray believe you have received it and you will."

Here is an imaginary act which has no support in fact. The tree was not withered at the time it was cursed, but when they returned the next day the imaginal act had been executed. So you see: this law is not limited to being constructive only. It can be used for good, bad, or indifferent purposes; for there are no limitations placed on the possibilities of prayer.

Now when you pray you must immerse yourself in the feeling of the wish fulfilled, for the word "pray" means, "Motion towards; accession to; at or in the vicinity of." Point yourself towards the wish fulfilled and accept that invisible state as reality. Then go your way knowing the desire is now yours. You did it and you will not be surprised when it comes to pass. When you first practice this technique you will be surprised when it happens; but when you learn how to completely accept the state assumed, you will know you do not have to do a thing to make it come to pass, as the assumption contains its own plan of fulfillment. You will know that this world is imaginal and that an assumption . . with no external object to support its truth . . will harden into fact when its truth is persisted in.

If an imaginal act produces an external fact to support it, then is not this world essentially imagined? If you dare to assume what your reason and senses deny and walk faithful to your assumption, believing in its reality . . and its corresponding effect is produced, can this seemingly solid, real world be anything other than imaginal? Everything is imagined, for you are God . . all imagination! God exists in you and you in Him. The world is all that you have imagined it to be, even though you cannot remember when or how you brought it into being.

You cannot feed the mind violence and not expect violence in the world. Although the networks will deny this, a friend at NBC-TV studio told me that when it was official that Kennedy was dead, he received an order from New York that for the next four days no violent films were to be shown. He said pandemonium took place in the studio, as they went through their files trying to find enough non-violent film to cover four days! Lucky for them, most of the time will be taken up with the giant coverage of the funeral in New York City.

One gentleman recently interviewed on television said that Senator Kennedy was always talking about being assassinated. That when the shots rang out, he instantly knew that Kennedy was dead. You cannot entertain thoughts of being assassinated without experiencing them. Who knows who, unseen by mortal eyes, was treading in the winepress, influencing that young boy's mind! Do not allow anyone to act as an intermediary between you and your God, for He is within you! God is never so far off as even to be near, for nearness implies separation. How can you be near God, when He became aware of being you? The moment He bestowed his spirit upon you, He gave you his consciousness, that you may . . by that consciousness . . understand the gift you have been given.

God gave me the gift of birth and Fatherhood. Without the gift of his spirit, I could not understand the gifts which have followed. How could I ever interpret the gift of belief or be awakened from my long sleep, if He who interprets all things had not first become me?

The Story of Jesus Is Persistent Assumption

When Pharaoh's butler and baker had dreams, they spoke to a slave, saying: "We had a dream." Joseph then replied: "Does not the interpretation belong to God? Tell me the dream." Now I ask you, is Joseph not claiming here that he is God?

The Book of Genesis begins: "In the beginning God" and ends "In a coffin in Egypt." Who is in the coffin? Joseph! So in the beginning God, as Joseph, is placed in a coffin in Egypt.

Now, having said that interpretation belongs to God, Joseph then interpreted their dreams. Two years later, he interpreted Pharaoh's dream and it came to pass, just as he said it would. If this story is true, is not the spirit of God upon man? Yes! Because God actually became as you are, that you may be as He is. Accept this literally, for it is true.

Imagination truly creates out of nothing! Thoughts call forth a thing that is not seen, as though it were happening. This is accomplished by an imaginal concept touched by feeling. Hearing of the success of another and feeling their joy builds a structure which will project itself on the screen of space. Calling the projection reality, one may think it was created from the outside. But what happened had to happen as it did, for there are no accidents. Last night Kennedy could have used other exits but he had to use the one he did, for there is a time for every imaginal act to project itself, just as there is a time to be born and a time to die, a time to laugh and a time to cry.

In Shakespeare's 'Macbeth' he described this world as a tale told by an idiot, full of sound and fury, signifying nothing. All realized ambitions are full of sound and fury, signifying nothing; for the real play takes place unseen by mortal eye and unheard of by mortal ear. The drama of life unfolds from within, for God the Father is molding you into his likeness. So set your hope fully upon this grace, this gift God gives of himself to you as he unfolds his image in you. All else is nothing more than sound and fury, meaning nothing!

Stalin's daughter, writing about her life in Russia and her father's death, told of a stroke which paralyzed one side of his body. Although his eyes were open, she doubted he saw anyone in the room; yet the expression on his face was that of extreme hatred. One arm was extended as though cursing what he saw. No one will know what Stalin was seeing for, "No one knows the thoughts of a man but the spirit of man which is in him." One can only speculate. Perhaps in that flashing moment he saw his dream of life crumble into ashes, and cursed the vision.

Now, in the eyes of millions Stalin was considered a very wise man, yet the Bible describes such a mind as a fool, saying: "The fool says in his heart there is no God." Show me a man who believes there is no God and . . although he may have many degrees and considered to be a very wise person . . he is a fool of fools.

The Bible does not imply that the uneducated man is the fool, only he who says in his heart there is no God. Stalin's world collapsed as the doors opened and he departed this little sphere. His world was real until that moment, and yet it was a world of fiction.

Everything here will collapse, but because this is a fictitious world you can have anything you want. Would you like to be known? To fulfill a great ambition? To be famous in the eyes of others? You can have them all, if you are willing to assume they are already yours. And, in spite of the evidence of your senses and the contradiction of your reason, if you walk and sleep in your assumption it will harden into fact. And after you have experienced them you will depart, leaving them all behind.

Your desire is brought into being by an imaginal act. It is sustained by an imaginal act, and when that imaginal act is withdrawn (or modified) your desire . . fulfilled . . will collapse and vanish. So I maintain there is no fiction!

A friend sent me a copy of the June issue of Harper's Magazine, which tells of a trial of a captain in our Air Force. As a school project this captain wrote an essay entitled, "Captain Dale Norte Has Been Court-martialed," in which he stated the place and the time it happened.

The Story of Jesus Is Persistent Assumption

Years later while in the Air Force, Captain Dale Norte was court-martialed, sentenced to a year of hard labor, and discharged from the service. Captain Norte wrote his own court-martial and then fulfilled it . . so what is fiction? You can write your own essay on success if that is your desire, and to the degree that you are self-persuaded it is true, you will give it life in your world.

The secret is to imagine to the point of self-persuasion. Can you believe what you are imagining? There are not two of you . . you and Imagination! You are not reshaping a piece of pottery when you imagine, but yourself! You are moving into your desire. If you persist until you see exactly what you want to see, fix your position with the glue of feeling and remain there . . it will be reflected on the screen of space, just as your world is now reflecting the fixed state from which you are viewing it.

There are two worlds: the outer world of effect and the inner world of causation. That inner world, in the depth of your soul, is where the true drama of life goes on. It is there that God is endowing you with life-giving power. Now a living soul, you are being transformed into a life-giving spirit!

On that day you will see this world from above, to discover it is dead and you are its animating power. Blake said: "Where man is not, nature is barren." This is true, for nature cannot produce anything by itself. Man, a living soul, causes things to appear alive by his animating power.

Although you are now animating all that you behold, you are destined to become a life-giving spirit . . to fashion things in your own image, bring them forth, and endow them with the power to create life. Believe me, there is no fiction! Every thought you think will come to pass. You may think it is just a thought and will never become real, but it will. Think you are a martyr, and you are. And you will continue to be one until you change your thinking. The Kennedy's, believing they are martyrs, will have these blows repeated over and over again until they awaken from within. I don't care how good your life seems to be at the moment, it is a dream from which you must . . and will . . awaken.

The Story of Jesus Is Persistent Assumption

What do you love the most . . your husband, wife, or child? It could even be some inanimate object that you treasure, yet one day you will have to tell it goodbye. Recently a lady showed me an enormous diamond ring she was wearing, saying she had paid $75,000 for it. Although she has children and grandchildren, this ring is so important to her, and she is so proud of it. Well, you could multiply this lady by millions who love objects that are dead, because they do not know that they are. Since we are living in a world of Caesar live it to the fullest, but do not be in love with it. Do not be moved by its emotions, as one million people were today as they watched a closed box, not knowing for sure a body was in it.

Now, the Bible teaches that permissible lies are allowed. An assumption not based upon fact is a lie, is it not? We are told to emulate the story of the unjust steward who . . when told he might lose his job . . asked the one who owed one hundred measures of oil to give him fifty, another eighty, and still another sixty. And when he returned to his master the steward was commended for his wisdom. This steward falsified the record, the facts of life which memory claimed to be correct. Perhaps memory says you only have ten dollars in the bank, the rent is due, and there are no prospects of more money on its way. Or that your friend is ill or out of a job. These are facts memory has recorded. You can falsify that record by a permissible lie, by seeing a thousand dollars in the bank and the rent as paid. By seeing one who is ill . . as well, or one who is unemployed . . as gainfully employed.

That which appears so real is based on fiction anyway, and fiction is fact in the sense that it is all imagination! You can lift anyone out of the state into which he has fallen and place him in another, be it a state of want, illness, or failure. There are infinite states into which man may fall.

If you will but believe that imagining creates reality, and there is no fiction, you can rewrite your life and give yourself and those within it beauty for ashes, gladness for mourning, and praise for fainthearted. Believe in the reality of your unseen act, then watch it fulfill itself. If you have proof that imagining creates reality, it will not matter what others

The Story of Jesus Is Persistent Assumption

think. All that matters is that you try it and allow imagination to prove himself in performance.

I encourage you to live as fully and as graciously as you desire to, while you wait for God's Son to reveal himself in you. But don't think that because you do not live fully and well, you are better off in the eyes of your Father . . for you are not. He is only interested in the work He is doing in you; and when it is completed, you will be born from within, for until that happens you cannot enter the kingdom of God. On that day you will enter an entirely different age, where trees, fruit, beasts, and birds are unknown, yet not unperceived. It is a world beyond other seas, unknown and inconceivable to those who live in this world of death.

When I say everything is at your disposal, I mean everything is in your imagination, and you are its creative power. Living in this fabulous world, you can travel unknown seas by gondola and know fruit, trees, birds, and beasts unknown here on earth; and in that world you are in complete control.

While walking the earth, man is totally unaware of the food he is mentally eating. Thoughts of horror and anger, jealousy and hate, feed invisible monsters which produce heartaches and pain. There are those who want the spoiled fruit which is part of this age; but when you enter that age, you are in complete control of your power. You realize that everything is a thought and under your control.

We are told: "Eye has not seen, ear has not heard and it has not entered into the heart of man the things already prepared by God for those who love him." When you are one with your Father, you will awaken to find yourself in that age which has already been prepared for you. So set your heart fully upon that world which you will enter at the unveiling of Christ from within.

As you awaken, one after the other, no two will have a duplicate experience. The symbolism will be there however, as well as the time element. It is always five months between the vision of the birth and the revelation of God's son.

The Story of Jesus Is Persistent Assumption

In the story recorded in the 40th chapter of the Book of Genesis, Joseph gave different interpretations to the number three in both dreams. The baker had three baskets on his head, with birds eating the bread contained therein. Joseph interpreted the dream by saying: "In three days you will hang from a tree and the birds will eat upon your flesh," and it came to pass as he interpreted it. The butler saw a vine with three branches which budded, blossomed, and ripened into grapes. He put the grapes into a cup, crushed them, and gave the cup to Pharaoh. The most important thing here is the grape vessel. Anyone can poison wine, so the cup bearer must be a trusted servant. It is he who drinks the wine first, and if poisoned, he dies and not the master.

Joseph interpreted the dream saying that the butler (the cup bearer) would be restored in three days, and he was. Now if it takes the spirit of God to interpret all dreams and all dreams come from God, is not he who interprets the dream the awakened man called Jesus Christ?

Remember, regardless of what happened today or what the future looks like, there is no fiction. Imagination creates its own reality. You have the power to change your present and your future by writing a glorious tale about yourself and those you love. Make it a first-person, present tense experience or as something you have already accomplished, and then live in that state, for imaging does create reality.

The stories I have spoken of come from the eleventh chapter of the Book of Mark. This entire chapter supports my theory. I urge you to have faith in God! He is not on the outside. He is not even near, because God actually becomes you! You will know you are He, when God's son, David, calls you Father. I can tell you that from now until the end of time God became you, but only when his son calls you Father, will you know who you really are.

In the meanwhile, believe me and test your creative power. You can bring anything out of nothing by conceiving a scene implying the fulfillment of a dream, and believing in its reality. Persist in your belief and your invisible dream will become a visible fact. That is falsifying the records . . which is allowed.

We are called upon to emulate the unjust steward. The word steward originally meant "the keeper of the pig," the symbol of Jesus Christ, the human imagination! You are the steward of your imagination. Feed it loving thoughts for yourself and others. If you feed on violence, you will become violent, for you become what you eat.

Born in the little island of Barbados, we kept ducks and chickens for our own consumption. If mother wanted a pair of ducks for a Sunday dinner, ten days prior she would tell one of her nine sons to put a brace of ducks aside.

Now, our ducks were raised in the yard and fed on fish, which was cheap and plentiful . . and not on corn, which had to be imported and was very expensive. We could buy a bucket of fish scraps for a penny, so we fed the chickens and ducks fish; consequently they smelled of and tasted like fish.

But if they were separated ten days or two weeks before you wanted them for dinner, and stuffed with corn and food of that nature, the entire texture of their flesh changed. During that interval of time however, they could not be given even a little bit of fish. They had to have a complete, radical change of diet.

If mother's command was not remembered until perhaps four days before the meal everyone knew it, because when the birds were plucked and the heat began to express the birds, the entire neighborhood knew the Goddard's were having fish for dinner, and no one could eat them. But if their diet was changed from fish to corn . . and only corn for that interval of time . . we had delicious ducks for dinner which tasted like ducks!

Now, although we are not ducks we do feed on ideas. Feed your mind a certain idea for one week and you will change its structure. Continue for two weeks and you will be well fed on lovely thoughts. You see, this is a fictitious world and you are its author. Nothing is impossible! It's all fiction anyway, so live nobly and dream beautiful dreams; for you are all imagination, and your human imagination is the Lord God, Jesus . . the Christ.

The Story of Jesus Is Persistent Assumption

Complete Lecture

The Secret Of Prayer . . 10-06-1967

The secret of scriptural prayer, as told in the form of a parable, is to pray and never lose heart. One such parable tells of a widow who kept coming to a judge, asking for vindication. At first he did not respond, then he said to himself: "Although I neither fear God, nor regard man, yet I will exonerate her, because by her much coming, she wearies me." Parables, like dreams, contain a single jet of truth. This parable urges persistence in mastering the art of prayer. Once you have mastered it you will live in the state of thanksgiving, and all through the day you will say over and over again to yourself: "Thank you, Father."

A most effective prayer is found in the 11th chapter of the Book of John, as: "Father, I thank thee that thou hast heard me, for thou always hears me." In this chapter, the story is told of someone who has died and has seemingly gone from this world. But the truth is that no one is dead to you, when you know how to pray. You may no longer touch, see, or hear those you love with your mortal senses; but if you know how to give thanks, you can move from your body of darkness into the world of light and encounter your loved ones there. Therefore, he who would learn how to pray will discover the great secret of a full and happy life.

In the 33rd chapter of the Book of Genesis, Jerusalem is called "Shechem." It is said that, "Jacob came safely into the city of Shechem, which is in the land of Canaan. There he erected an altar and called it El Elohey Israel, which means "the God of Israel". Orienting himself toward Shechem (the true direction) Jacob remained in El Elohey Israel, which means "safe in mind, body, or estate".

We are told that Daniel oriented himself at an open window, where he looked toward Jerusalem. And those in the Mohammedan world pray looking towards what they call Mecca. But because Christianity takes place within, scripture is speaking of the Jerusalem within, and not on the outside at all. When you pray you do not prostrate yourself on the ground and look towards some eastern point in space, but adjust yourself mentally into your fulfilled desire. Although this technique is simple, it takes practice to become its master. Your true direction is to the knowledge of what you want. Knowing your desire, point yourself directly in front of it by thinking from its fulfillment. Silence all thought and allow the doors of your mind to open. Then enter your desire. Stay with your imagination as your companion. Start by thinking of your imagination as something other than yourself, and eventually you will know you are what you formerly called your imagination. It is possible to amputate a hand, leg, or various parts of the body . . but imagination cannot be amputated, for it is your eternal Self!

Let me show you what I mean. While standing here in Los Angeles, I may desire to be elsewhere. Time and finances may not allow it, but in my imagination I can assume I am already there. Now, by a mere act of assumption on my part, God departs this body. If I assume I am in New York City, anyone I think of in Los Angeles must be three thousand miles away. No longer can I think of them as just down the street or in the hills west of me. That is my test.

The word "prayer" means "motion towards, accession to, at or in the vicinity of". Orienting myself towards New York City, I have made a motion, an accession to. As I act in the vicinity of, I see my friends relative to New York City. Having done this, let me have full confidence in my imagination, knowing he is the being who made the motion. Blake's words are true: "Man is all Imagination, and God is Man and exists in us and we in Him. Man's Immortal Body is the Imagination, and that is God Himself."

You can not only move in space but also in time and fulfill your every desire. Prayer does not have to be confined to what a person calls self. You can pray for another by feeling they now have what they formerly wanted, for feeling is a movement. The first creative act recorded in scripture is motion: "God moved upon the face of the water."

The Story of Jesus Is Persistent Assumption

A friend recently had a fantastic vision, during which he asked: "Did I learn anything?" and I answered: "Yes. You learned how to move." Then everything was transformed, as conflict deceased, a hovel became a castle, the battlefield a sea of ripened wheat, and he was escorted into his eternal home. Prayer is motion. It is learning how to move toward a change in your bank balance, your marital status, or social world. Learn to master the art of motion; for after you move, change begins to rise up out of the deep. The technique of prayer is mastering your inner motion. If you are seeing things you would like to change, move in your imagination to the position you would occupy after the change took place.

Everything and everyone in your world is yourself pushed out. Any request from another . . heard by you . . should not be ignored; for it is coming from yourself! You came down from a world of light to confine yourself to this body of darkness. Now a spark from an infinite world of light, one day you will remember that world and awaken, but in the meantime you must learn to exercise the power of your mind. Having remembered the infinite world of light, I now know that everything is myself, as all things are contained within me.

Prayer is psychological movement. It is the art of moving from a problem to its solution. When a friend calls, telling of a problem, we hang up, and I move from the problem state to its solution by hearing the same lady tell me the problem is now solved. A friend recently shared this dream with me: We were in a garden and he told me all of his desires, when I said: "Don't desire them, live them!" This is true. Desire is thinking of! Living is thinking from! Don't go through life desiring. Live your desire. Think it is already fulfilled. Believe it is true; for an assumption, though false, if persisted in will harden into fact.

When you are learning the art of prayer, persistence is necessary, as told us in the story of the man who . . coming at night . . said: "Friend, lend me three loaves of bread." Although his friend replied: "It is late, the door is closed, my children are in bed, and I cannot come down and serve you," because of the man's importunity, his friend gave him what he wanted. The word importunity means brazen impudence. The man repeated and repeated his request, unwilling to take no for an answer. The same is true in the story of the widow. These are all parables told to illustrate prayer.

The Lord's Prayer teaches the oneness of us all. It begins: "Our Father." If God is our Father, are we not one? Regardless of our race or color of skin, if we have a common Father, we must have a common brotherhood.

Eventually we are all going to know we are the Father; but in the meanwhile, persistence is the key to a change in life . . more income, greater recognition, or whatever the desire may be. If your desire is not fulfilled today, tomorrow, next week or next month . . persist, for persistency will pay off. All of your prayers will be answered if you will not give up.

My old friend, Abdullah, gave me this exercise. Every day I would sit in my living room where I could not see the telephone in the hall. With my eyes closed, I would assume I was in the chair by the phone. Then I would feel myself back in the living room. This I did over and over again, as I discovered the feeling of changing motion. This exercise was very helpful to me. If you try it, you will discover you become very loose with this exercise. Practice the art of motion, and one day you will discover that by the very act of imagining, you are detached from your physical body and placed exactly where you are imagining yourself to be . . so much so that you are seen by those who are there.

Being all imagination, you must be wherever you are in imagination. Moving in your imagination, you are preparing a place for your desires to be fulfilled. Then you return, to walk through a series of events which will lead you up to where you have placed yourself. In imagination, I can put myself where I desire to be. I move and view the world from there. Then I return here, confident that . . in a way unknown to me . . this being who can do all things and knows all things, will lead me physically across a bridge of incident up to where I have placed myself.

The Story of Jesus Is Persistent Assumption

You can move in imagination to any place and any time. Dwell there as though it were true, and you will have learned the secret of prayer.

My wife had a wonderful vision where she found herself in a grove of trees. Walking down a clear passage, she saw people gathered around an altar. A lady approached, carrying a book entitled, The Credence of Faith and the Forgiveness of Sins according to Judaism. Reaching the altar, she began to read it aloud. Shortly, another lady appeared, carrying a book entitled, The Credence of Faith and the Forgiveness of Sins according to Christianity. Approaching the altar, she too opened her book and began to read. As my wife listened, she realized it was infinitely more difficult to be a Christian than to be a Jew. She saw the whole thing was psychological. That nothing is done on the outside, because everything comes from within.

Browning began his wonderful poem, "Easter Day" with the words: "How hard it is to be a Christian." And Chapman said: "Christianity has not been tried and proved wanting. It has been tried and found difficult and therefore given up." Why? Because a Christian cannot pass the buck and blame another. Christianity is built upon the foundation that all are one. That man is forever drawing conformation of what he is doing within himself. That your world bears witness to what you are doing to yourself. This is difficult to accept, yet it is Christianity. No man comes unto me, save my Father who sent me calls him. I and my Father are one, therefore I call all those who enter my life to reveal to me what I am doing in my imagination. Learn how to pray. Master it and make your world conform to the ideal you want to experience.

Stop thinking of, and start thinking from. To think from the wish fulfilled is to realize that which you will never experience while you are thinking of it. When you put yourself into the state of the wish fulfilled and think from it, you are praying, and in a way your reasoning mind does not know, your wish will become a fact in your world. You can be the man or woman you want to be, when you know how to pray. All things are possible to him who believes, therefore learn the art of believing and persuade yourself it is true.

The Story of Jesus Is Persistent Assumption

Then one day, occupying space and time in your imagination, you will be seen by another, who will call or send you a letter verifying your visit. This I know from experience.

The Bible is not just beautiful poetry; it is the inspired word of God. Written by poets, they have given enlarged meaning to normal words. When you put your body on the bed and assume you are elsewhere, are you not all imagination? In the act of imagining, you depart the dark caverns of this body and appear where you imagine yourself to be, because you are God . . all imagination . . and cannot die. You cannot go to eternal death in that which cannot die, and your immortal being is imagination! You are the central being of scripture . . the one called Jesus Christ, who is the Lord God Jehovah . . who descended here for a purpose.

While here, you must pay the price of living in the world of Caesar. You may criticize our politicians and protest any raise in taxes, but you will continue to be taxed. All you have to do is learn the art of prayer and make more money.

I am reminded of a story told of the late President Kennedy. It seems his father . . who had, in one generation, made something like four-hundred million dollars . . complained that his children were spending too much money. At a banquet, President Kennedy said: "The only solution to this problem is for father to make more money."

One day a friend told me that when she was a child, her father would say: "If you have but a dollar and it was necessary for you to spend it, do so as if it were a dry leaf, and you the owner of a boundless forest." If one really knows how to pray, he could spend his dollar and then reproduce it again. You see, this world is brought into being by man's imagination, so it is very important to learn the secret of prayer.

If you are still desiring, stop it right now! Ask yourself what it would be like, were your desire a reality. How would you feel if you were already the one you would like to be? The moment you catch that mood, you are thinking from it. And the great secret of prayer is thinking from, rather than thinking of. Anchored here, you know where you live, your bank balance, job, creditors, friends, and loved ones . . as you are thinking from this state. But you can move to another state and give it the same sense of reality, when you find and practice the great secret of prayer.

Take my message to heart and live by it. Practice the art of prayer daily, and then one day you will find the most effective prayer is: "Thank you Father." You will feel this being within you as your very self. You can speak of it as "thou" yet know it is "I." You will then have a thou/I relationship, and say to yourself: "Thank you, Father". If I want something, I know the desire comes from the Father, because all thought springs from Him. Having given me the urge, I thank Him for fulfilling it. Then I walk by faith, in confidence that he who gave it to me through the medium of desire will clothe it in bodily form for me to encounter in the flesh.

Don't get in the habit of judging and criticizing, seeing only unlovely things. You have a life . . live it nobly. It is so much easier to be noble, generous, loving, and kind, than to be judgmental. If others want to do so, let them. They are an aspect of yourself that you haven't overcome yet, but don't fall into that habit. Simply thank your heavenly Father over and over and over again, because in the end, when the curtain comes down on this wonderful drama, the supreme actor will rise from it all and you will know that you are He.

Complete Lecture

Persistent Assumption . . 03-18-1968

I tell you a truth: There is nothing greater than your own wonderful human imagination! It is He who inspired Blake, Shakespeare, and Einstein, for there is only one spirit in the universe! "Hear, O Israel, the Lord our God, the Lord is One." That one spirit is the human imagination! When Blake was asked what he thought of the divinity of Christ he answered: "Christ is the only God, but so AM I and so are you." Don't think of Christ as someone greater than yourself. He is the only God, but so AM I and so are you! Don't consider yourself less than Christ, for there is only God, who is your own wonderful human imagination.

Daring to assume that all things are possible to imagine, put this one reality to the extreme test by assuming you are the person you would like to be. Your reasonable mind and outer senses may deny it; but I promise you: if you will persist, you will receive your assumption. Believe me, you are the same God who created and sustains the universe, but are keyed low; so you must be persistent if you would bring about a change.

In the Book of Luke, the story is told of a man who came to a house at the midnight hour, and said: "A friend has arrived who is hungry. Would you let me have three loaves of bread?" The man upstairs replied: "It is midnight. My children are in bed asleep and I cannot come down and give you what you want." Then this statement is made: "But because of the man's importunity, he was given all that he desired." The word "importunity" means "brazen impudence." Having a desire, the man would not take no for an answer!

When you know what you want, you don't ask God as though he were another; you ask your individual self to bring about your desire, for you are he! And God . . your own wonderful human imagination . . will respond when you will not take no for an answer, as your denial is spoken from within and there is no other. It is within your own being that you persist in assuming you have received what you want.

The Story of Jesus Is Persistent Assumption

The story is, even though it was midnight and the family was asleep, the father came down and gave what was needed.

The God of a Blake, a Shakespeare, or an Einstein, does not differ from the God housed in you, as there is only one human imagination. There cannot be two. He is not a dual God. You and your imagination are not less than anyone, but you must learn to be persistent.

A friend recently shared a vision with me, in which I appeared and said: "The story of Jesus is persistent assumption." If this is true, and we are told to imitate him as a dear child, I must dare to assume I am the being I want to be. I must continue in that assumption until that which I have assumed is objectively realized. And if I am one with everyone, how can anyone be greater than I? Do not believe that someone is greater than you because of some influx of spirit or validity. Your imagination is the only God, and there is no other being greater than He! Claim you are what you want to be. Persist in that assumption. Continue to assume that role until that which you have assumed is reflected in your world.

Although the churches teach that another, greater than yourself, said: "Unless you believe that I AM He, you will die in your sins" . . these words were spoken by the human imagination! And because imagination is one, and you can't get away from that oneness, don't think of another. Accept these words in the first person, present tense; for unless you believe that you already are what you want to be, you will die in your sins by leaving your desire unfulfilled. If you do not believe you are all imagination, you will continue in your former belief, worshipping a God on the outside and not within.

On this level, we are fragmented, but we are all that one imagination. The word "Elohim" is a compound unity of one made up of others. Although we seem to be many, in the most intimate manner possible, we are one! On this level, you and I are keyed low for purposes beyond our wildest dreams, yet called upon to make the effort to rise above it. This is done in a physical, scientific, and artistic sense, as we begin to discover and express our human imagination. We rise above this level through the act of assumption; for an assumption, though false, if persisted in will harden into fact. As William Blake said: "If the fool will persist in his folly he will become wise."

There is nothing God cannot do! Do not think that one who is fabulously rich has an influx of spirit which differs from yours. He is imagining wealth, either wittingly or unwittingly; but you can do it knowingly. If he does not know what he is doing, he can lose his wealth and not know how to recover it. I am asking you, regardless of your financial situation, to assume wealth, knowingly. If, tomorrow you would again return to your former state, bring wealth back by claiming "I AM wealthy," for there is only one God. He who creates poverty also creates wealth, as there is no other creator.

The world thinks of numberless gods, but there is only one. That one is your own wonderful human imagination. Possessing only one son, when imagination awakens, God's only begotten son will reveal you as God. The same thing will happen to another, then another . . and eventually everyone will see the same son, who will reveal the individual as God the Father.

This world is a play, where divine imagination becomes human imagination by inserting himself into an olive skin, a black skin, a white skin, and a red skin. Although we appear to be different, we all will see God's only begotten son . . proving that there is only one God. The purpose behind the play is to expand imagination's creative power. Here we are fragmented into numberless parts, destined to gather ourselves together into the one God, the one Father of all.

Begin now to actively, constantly, use your imagination; for as you prove its creative power on this level, you are awakening to a higher level and birth into the spirit world where you know yourself to be God. Prove to yourself that you are God by feeling your desire is now an accomplished fact. Listen to your friends talk about you. Are they rejoicing because of your good fortune, or are they expressing envy? Imagine their words are true. Persist in imagining they are true. Continue to imagine your desire is already an accomplished fact; and when it is objectively realized, proof will be yours.

Think of something lovely you would like to give another. Then ask yourself if you gave it to him and he wouldn't accept it, would you want to keep it for yourself? If, for instance, you gave a friend a million dollars and he would not accept it, would you be willing to keep it? I'm sure you would. Then imagine giving the money to him, then give to others in the same way. You may not even have a bank account; but you can still give, because there is no one to give to but yourself! There is only God whose name is I AM!

"Hear, O Israel, the Lord our God, the Lord is one." This great confession of faith is recorded in the sixth chapter, the fourth verse of the Book of Deuteronomy. The Lord is not two, not a dozen . . just one. If I say "I AM" that's one, but if I say "we are" I am speaking of many.

Jesus' name is "I AM." He is not some superior being other than yourself. He is the inspiration for everything you write, be it trivia or profound. Inspiration does not come from some other being, because there cannot be another. When you sit down to write, the thoughts come from your own being! It is nonsense to think of some other being as possessing you.

The great poets . . the Shakespeare's, the Blake's . . had no great spiritual influx moving in them that is greater than the spiritual influx in you. It cannot be, for there is no one greater than self! When someone tells me he is under the influence of some greater power, I tell him that is not possible. The inspiration is coming from the depths of his own soul. Perhaps you have an item you would like to advertise. As you think of what your customer needs, the answer will come from the depth of your own soul, and you will know what needs to be said to promote your product. You do not receive some influx of spirit outside of yourself, for there is no one greater! There is only God, and God is one!

The Story of Jesus Is Persistent Assumption

In the Book of Psalms, you are told to; "Commune with your own self." Sit quietly. Be at peace with yourself and suddenly thoughts will begin to flow within you, from God. In the beginning you were God! And in the end, you and I and the whole vast world of billions will be re-gathered into the one God. One imagination fell into this fragmented world of seeming others, yet the whole is within each one of us. A man's enemies are those of his own household, for they are all within him. Not knowing this, man fights within himself until he realizes there is no other, just himself. Then he tells others in the hope he can convince himself. And as he rises from within, he is called back into the one being he was before that the world was. The fall into division was deliberate for God's expansion into unity.

There was no other way to expand your creative power but by falling into limitation and overcoming it. As you fell, your being fragmented. I saw this so clearly in vision. First, a rock appeared. Then it fragmented and as it gathered together it took the shape of a man sitting in the lotus posture, meditating, glowing. And I knew I was looking at myself! And as it began to glow like the sun, I awoke in my apartment in New York City.

I am telling you what I have done, what I have seen, and what I have experienced. Each one of us has a being within who is meditating us. The being in you and the being in all, form the one perfect being, who fell and fragmented himself. One day, everyone's living being will unite into the one God, who fell and fragmented himself. Do you know what you would you like to be? Dare to assume it and, for one week, claim: "I have assumed I am the one I want to be. I am still assuming I am, and I will continue to assume I am until that which I have assumed is objectively realized." Fall asleep assuming it is true, and let that living being in you give it life.

God the Father is dreaming in the depth of your soul. It is he who began a good work in you, and it is he who will bring it to completion at the day of Jesus Christ. On that day you will be brought to the same perfection as the Father in you, for God is dreaming himself into a greater image of himself and you, the dreamer, are dreaming yourself into the image of yourself.

While you are here, you can assume any desire for yourself and those you love. Then you can dare to believe in what you have assumed. And if you continue your assumption, you will express it. But you must believe, or you will die in your sins. Always talking to yourself, you are telling yourself that unless you believe you are the man you want to be, you will remain being the man you don't want to be, thereby dying in your sins.

To believe in another . . whether he appear as a Blake, a Shakespeare or an Einstein . . you have a false God. You must believe in yourself or die in your sins! You must believe that God actually became you that you may become God . . for he did. His name is I AM and unless you say within yourself: "I AM what I want to be" and believe it, you will remain saying within yourself: "I wish I were what I want to be" and die in your frustration (your sin). I urge to you learn how to believe in yourself. It may appear to be difficult at first, but not when you are willing to go out on a limb and try it.

I admire the great, inspired poets. Shakespeare is marvelous. Blake is altogether wonderful, and Einstein truly great in his field. These were inspired men; but they did not have any influx of spirit that made them greater than your human imagination, for their imagination and your imagination are one grand, divine imagination, imagining! Their work did not come from something outside of themselves, but from their own imagination, awakening. That same imagination is yours because there is only one spirit. The spirit of man is one with the spirit of the universe and there is no other!

Start now to capture the feeling of being this one spirit. Fall asleep in the feeling that you are God, and as you come hurtling back from the depth of unconsciousness toward this level, you will have numberless crazy little dreams based upon this person you are coming through. You will give importance to these dreams; but oh, what depths you will reach in that which is unconscious relative to this level!

Let no one frighten you, for you are an immortal being who cannot die. Although I have awakened to my Godhood before you, I am no better because I got there first, for there is no such thing as being first. Everyone is moving toward that level, and no one can fail. And when all have returned, what joy will be expressed as we form the one body, the one spirit, the one Lord, the one God and Father of all! Everyone will have the vision and prove to himself that he is God the Father.

I urge you to apply this principle and cushion yourself against the normal blows of life. If your friends and loved ones cannot believe, cushion them anyway; for no matter what you leave them here, you are not going to stop the blows given by the depth of their own being. If you left each friend one hundred thousand dollars, you would cushion them for the moment; but the depth of their being will continue to take them through experiences, in order to awaken to the knowledge that they are the father of God's only begotten son, David.

The world is searching for the cause of the phenomena of life, not knowing he is their very self. What responsibility is yours when you discover that your awareness is the cause of everything that has happened, is happening, and will happen to you. But when you realize that you are causing all the blows, the heartaches, and pains, that happen to you, you will begin to change your thinking; and as you do, scripture will unfold in you.

Now let us go into the Silence.

The Story of Jesus Is Persistent Assumption

Complete Lecture

Persistent Assumption .. 06-18-1968

Now, you and I look out on a world, and we think of the great men and women who are publicized in the world, and many of them are altogether wonderful. We speak of the great poets, the scientists, the businessmen .. all these fellows in the world, and we think, "Well now, there must be something different about them."

Now, may I tell you? There's not a thing different about them. I want to convince you this night, if I can, that this inspiration that we think the poet has, the scientist, the great businessman, is not an influx of a spirit that is different. It's not different from the individual's own wonderful human imagination, because there's nothing greater. So, there is no greater influx of Spirit into a Blake, into a Shakespeare, into an Einstein, into you, than your own wonderful human imagination, for there is nothing greater. There is only one Spirit in man and the Universe!

"Hear, O Israel, the Lord our God, the Lord is one"

There is not a greater spirit than your own wonderful human imagination.

In a little conversation that Blake had with his friend, Crabb Robinson, Robinson asked him what he thought of the divinity of Christ and he answered, "Christ is the only God, but so am I, and so are you. Now don't forget it! When you think of Christ, you are making something bigger than yourself .. something greater than yourself. Blake said, "Christ is the only God, but so am I." If Christ is the only God "and so am I," I make myself one with him. Then he turns to Crabb Robinson and says, "So are you." So don't forget it.

If you forget this, you make yourself less than the One. You can't be less than the One; there is only One. There is only God in this world! There is nothing but God, and God is your own wonderful human imagination. That is God.

The Story of Jesus Is Persistent Assumption

Now tonight, let us put it to the extreme test. If God is the only Reality . . you can't have two, not two gods . . and He is my own wonderful human imagination, and "All things are possible to God." All right, how would I go about proving it? For I am called upon to test it!

"Test it." I will dare to assume that I am the man that I would like to be. At the moment, reason denies it, my senses deny it; but I will dare to assume that I am it. Now, what am I told in Scripture that I should do? Well, listen to it carefully. These are stories told in Scripture of the necessity of persistence because we are "keyed low." The same God . . the God that created the Universe and sustains it by His Creative Power . . is the God that is sitting here in these chairs tonight. But here for a divine purpose, the same God is "keyed low."

So, would I bring about a change in my world? Then I am called upon in Scripture to be persistent, because I see this world, and everything that I have assumed is denied . . as I assume it . . by the things round about me. Now listen to these stories as told in Scripture.

A man came at the midnight hour to his friend, and he said, "A friend has called, 'I have no bread. Would you just let me have three loaves of bread?' and the one who opened the upstairs window said to him, 'It is midnight, and my children are asleep in bed. I cannot come down and give you what you want.'"

And the story as told us in the book of Luke is this: he would not come down; but because of this man's importunity, he came down and gave him all that he needed. Well, the word translated importunity means brazen impudence. He would not take "No" for an answer.

I don't ask you, as an individual . . I don't ask any outside god; as an individual, I am asking my Self to bring this thing to pass. That is what I am actually saying, because I am speaking to the only God. There is only God! And if God is my own wonderful human imagination, to whom am I going

The Story of Jesus Is Persistent Assumption

to turn when It doesn't respond . . when I don't take "No" for an answer?

So, within my own being, I am assuming that I have received exactly what I need. Now the story is that even though it was midnight, he was in bed with his children, still he came down and gave him what he needed. You do not take "No" for an answer, because there is no "other," may I tell you? I don't care whether you speak of a Shakespeare whom you think, "My god, isn't he marvelous!" . . and he is; and the Blakes of the world, and they are marvelous; and the Einsteins, and they are marvelous. But the God of an Einstein does not differ from the God of your own wonderful human imagination. There is only God! There can't be two.

"Hear, O Israel, the Lord our God, the Lord is One." He is not a dual God . . one God. So, your own wonderful human imagination is this God, and you are not less than any being in this world. But you have to be persistent.

When Benny came home last night, he said, "Neville, have you forgotten my vision? When I was talking to someone and you came into the picture, and this one said to you . . and he asked this very simple question! 'Tell us the story of Jesus,' and you automatically said, 'The story of Jesus is persistent assumption.'"

Persistent assumption . . that's the story, for "Jesus" means "salvation." Well, if persistent assumption is the story of Jesus, I must dare to assume that I AM what I want to be. I must continue in the assumption that I AM it until that which I have assumed is objectively realized. That is the story of Jesus. For if I am one with anything in this world, and he is great and she is great, and I am not, and yet we are one, well, now . . what is this fragmented being when there is only one? I tell you, that One is your own wonderful human imagination, and don't let anyone in this world tell you that an Einstein or a Shakespeare is greater because of some influx of a spirit of greater validity than their own wonderful human imagination, because there is no greater. Your imagination is God, and there is no other God. And there can be no other greater Being than your own wonderful human imagination.

Now you begin to imagine it. Well, now I will say, "I have assumed that I am the man that I want to be." I am still assuming that I AM He, and I will continue to assume that I AM He until that which I have assumed is objectively realized, as told us in the 8th chapter of John:

"Unless you believe I AM He" . . now when you read it, you think as you are taught by the churches of the world, that another greater than yourself is speaking, it is not another greater than you speaking, telling you unless you believe He is . . it's your Self speaking. There is only God, because God is One and you can't get away from the Oneness: don't think of "another."

So, these words must be accepted in the first person, present tense, so "unless you believe that I AM He, you will die in your sins" . . you'll miss the mark. I must believe that I am the man that I want to be. If I do not believe that I am that very being so that I can say, "Well, I AM He," then I will continue what I formerly believed myself to be. This is the story of Scripture. So, we are all one . . everyone here. You and I are one, because there can't be two. On this level, for a purpose, we are fragmented; but I am sent to tell you that we are not really many. We are one.

The word "Elohim" is a compound unity: one made up of others. So here it seems to be "others," but you and I are not really two, three, four, or many. We are one, in the most intimate manner that you've ever known, without loss of identity!

So, I ask you this night to simply dwell upon it, and simply try it. Just try it. It will never in Eternity fail you.

Here is a letter that came to me this past week. She said in her letter, "I was awakened by the laughter of my husband. He was laughing . . the sweetest laughter I have ever heard . . just a laugh. I have never heard him laugh like this. So I awoke, and here he's laughing a peculiar but wonderful laughter. And I said to myself, 'Well, he's undoubtedly dreaming something that is altogether wonderful.'

"And then the next morning he said to me, 'I had the loveliest dream last night. I dreamt that you were telling me it's so easy to believe that I AM God.'"

Now I am going to tell him, . . he is here tonight alone; she isn't here . . tell her, and you too, read it: the 126th Psalm. There is your answer, only six verses. That was the laughter of God.

She said, "I heard a voice coming from within me saying, 'You've just heard the laughter of God!'"

Well, read the 126th Psalm, when all returned to Zion . . those who were left. They all left, and then they all are brought back into Zion, and here, you hear the laughter of God.

When the LORD restored the fortunes of Zion, We were like those who dream. 2Then our mouth was filled with laughter, And our tongue with shouts of joy; Then they said among the nations, "The LORD has done great things for them." 3 The LORD had done great things for us; we are glad. 4 Restore our fortunes, O LORD, Like the watercourses in the Negeb! 5 May those who sow in tears Reap with shouts of joy! 6 He that goes forth weeping, Bearing the seed for sowing, Shall come home with shouts of joy, Bringing his sheaves with him.

So, she heard him laugh in a way that she had never heard him before, and she had never heard this kind of a laughter. And she said to herself, "He's undoubtedly having a wonderful dream."

Then the next day he said to her, "I had a dream last night, and in my dream you were telling me that it is so easy to believe that I AM God!"

So, I tell you, you try it; this thing doesn't fail. There is only God. You are not something less than God; there is only God.

The Story of Jesus Is Persistent Assumption

And you and I, on this level, for purposes beyond the wildest dream . . we are keyed low; but we are called upon to make the effort to rise from this level. And so, we do it in a business sense, in a scientific sense, in an artistic sense; and so we begin to express this talent, which is our own wonderful human imagination, which is God. There is nothing but God!

So, I am called upon to assume that I am what I want to be, for, "An assumption, though false, if persisted in will harden into fact" [Sir Anthony Eden].

And as Blake said, "If the fool would persist in his folly, he would become wise" [from "The Marriage of Heaven and Hell"].

There is nothing that is impossible to God. So, don't say that something cannot be, . . I don't care what it is. You may see someone in the world, and he is a fabulously wealthy person. Well, so what! Do you think for one second some influx of Spirit that differs from the Being that you are, possessed him to make it? No. He either did it wittingly or unwittingly; may I tell you? But you can do it knowingly. If he does it unknowingly, which is the self, and he loses it tonight, he may not know how to recover it. I am asking you . . without having anything . . to do it knowingly.

So, should you tomorrow fall into another state, and you remember the story, you simply come back and simply bring it back into your world as you want it, and simply multiply it, and live graciously, for there's only one God, You can't conceive of . . well, you can conceive of a second god, but it is a stupid concept because there is no other god. When the world thinks of numberless gods, they are stupid. There's only one God, and that God is your own wonderful human imagination!

And the day will come that you will prove it. You will actually witness the One God! He sets Himself up at the very beginning, and this God has only one Son. And when you awaken and that Son calls you "Father" . . and therefore you are the father of the only Son of God . . well then, you know

The Story of Jesus Is Persistent Assumption

you are the only God! And then another one comes and another one comes; and eventually all come, and they see the same Son, and the same Son calls them "Father." Therefore, everyone is the same God the Father! And there aren't two of us.

There aren't two. Forget all the pigments of skin. All this is part of the "play." To put me into an olive skin and one in a black, black skin, and one in a white, white skin, and one in a red skin, it makes it appear as though we differ. And therefore, because we differ there must be different gods. And yet, all will have that same Son, and that one Son will call all of us . . regardless of sex . . "Father," proving that we are only one God. And the purpose behind it all is simply to create an expansion of His creative power.

So here we are scattered . . fragmented into numberless parts. And then all are gathered together into one God, one Father. I am going to ask you all to try it . . really try it, because if you really prove it on this level, may I tell you, you will never forget it! And you will be sustained by this level, and then, all of a sudden, you will be "born from above." I cannot tell you when, that is a secret hidden from us here.

If you tell me when you were "born from above," then I can tell you all the other events that will follow and when it will happen. I can tell you that because I have recorded it. But the actual "birth from above" remains a secret. "It comes like a thief in the night," but when it comes, you are "born from above," and you are God! You actually are God!

Now to prove that you are, you can create . . create in this simple, simple way: What would it be like if it were true? Just what would it be like? How would I feel if . . and then you name it. How would I feel if she, or he, were as I would like them to be? So, you would like something lovely to happen to them, and then you feel it.

Now, can you persist in that assumption? I imagine it to be so. I am still imagining it to be so, and I will continue to imagine that these things are as I have imagined them to be until it is objectively realized. Can I do that? Well, if I can,

The Story of Jesus Is Persistent Assumption

they will conform to it. Must I get their permission? I don't need their permission if we are one. That is what I want for them. I don't need their consent if it is something I would like for myself.

Always ask yourself, "Would I like it for myself?" If they reject it . . and they can reject it; but I mean, take it on this level. If they should reject it, would I willingly accept it? If I gave you a million dollars and you wouldn't take it, would I be willing to receive it again? I would. Well then, give it in that same way. And may I tell you? You can do it.

If you don't have one nickel in the bank . . if you don't have a bank account, you can do it, because there is no one but your Self. There is only God in this world. God is I AM. There is nothing but God!

"Hear, O Israel, the Lord our God, the Lord is One" . . the greatest prayer . . the greatest confession of faith that man could ever make. Read it in the 6th chapter of the book of Deuteronomy. I think it is the 4th verse. But oh! What a confession of faith!

"Hear, O Israel, the Lord our God, the Lord is One.

Not two, not a dozen . . just one.

Well, if He is One, what is One in this world? When I say, "I AM," that's one. If I say, "We are," that is multiple. But I AM, and that is His name. Don't forget it! Therefore, if I AM, even though, now, something is happening, I am not receiving from some superior being . . there is no superior being than my Self. The inspiration for anything I write . . if I sit down and write something that is all trivia or something that is altogether marvelous, it does not come from some other being who inspires me, because there is no greater Being. There cannot be another Being. So, when I sit down to write and I am in the mood, from my own Being it is coming out, and I am writing; but to say that some other Being is possessing me and they are taking over . . nonsense! No other Being: there can be no other Being.

So, the poet, the Shakespeares, the Blakes, the great writers of the world, or any writer in the world . . he doesn't have any Being influencing him, moving in some peculiar spiritual influx that is greater than himself. It cannot be. There is no one greater than himself. So, when someone tells me, "I was under the influence of something other than myself, it came from the outside" . . forget it. There isn't anyone; it's all coming from the depth of your own Soul.

So, all of a sudden, you are an advertiser, and you are sitting and wondering, "Now what does my customer need?" And all of a sudden, from the depths of your own Soul it comes . . what you are going to say to promote that product. It isn't some influx of a spirit other than your Self. It can't be, because there is nothing greater than your Self. There is no other god; there is only one God.

So, you sit, and you are communing with Self, as told you in the Psalms: "Commune with your own Self." Well, you can sit on a chair or on your bed and commune with your own Self and be at peace. And all of a sudden the thing begins to flow from within, because there is only one God. And everything unfolds from within you: there is nothing but God. And in the end, you and I and the whole vast world of billions will be re-gathered into one body . . and, oh, what a joy!

One fell purposely into this fragmented world, seeing "others". . and fighting seeming "others" and the horror within one's Self that a man's enemies are "of his own household," meaning himself. He is fighting with himself, not knowing that everything in this world is himself. All of a sudden he realizes, there is no other . . just himself! And then he knows it, and he tells everyone in this world, in the hope that he can convince himself, because it is himself he's talking to, for there's only one God . . only one Being.

And then as he rises within himself, he once more coalesces into the One Being, knowing in the depth of his Being that everyone is going to coalesce into the same Being, and oh what a joy when all are raised into the One Being that was that Being before the Fall, And the Fall was a deliberate fall for the expansion of its power.

The Story of Jesus Is Persistent Assumption

I can only expand my creative power by falling into this limitation and overcoming it. There is no other way to do it. And as I fell, I fragmented my being. I saw it so clearly in my vision; and the Being that fragmented was my Self . . I saw it. I saw this whole rock fragmented. It all gathered together. When I looked, I am looking at my Self . . a glowing Being like the sun glowing. I've never known that I could . . this little thing talking to you now.

Here every part of the body at my age . . naturally it gets older and parts disappear from it, and yet, I am looking at this Being sitting in a lotus posture and this fantastic beauty. I could hardly believe I could ever in Eternity equal that beauty! And yet I am looking at my Self! And here, this is His meditative world fragmented, and then it is all put back together, and I am looking at my Self. I can't tell you my thrill when I looked at it.

It was first a rock, and then the rock became fragmented. Then the rock was gathered together; but instead of being a rock, it's now a being . . a human being sitting in the lotus posture, meditating. And it's a glorious, beautiful being. I can't describe the beauty of that man; I'm looking at my Self! How can I ever be described as a man called Neville with such beauty? And yet, I am looking at my Self. Such majesty! Such strength of character, such power . . all woven into one being sitting in the lotus posture. And it glows and glows like a sun, and when it reaches the intensity of Power, it explodes. And then I awake here sitting in my apartment on 75th Street in New York City. That's why I am telling you what I know, what I've seen, what I have experienced. But that is true of everyone. You . . there is a Being in you that is meditating you. And the Being in you and the Being in me and the Being in all . . woven together . . form that Being that is the Ultimate God. And that Being is perfect. And may I tell you, I don't care what you've gone through . . you could lose your eyes, lose your hands, lose your feet, be dishonored in this world, but that Being that is meditating you is the most glorious Being you could ever conceive. You have never known such beauty.

The Story of Jesus Is Persistent Assumption

Oh, you can go to all the beauty parlors in the world, and they will bring you out and you will think, "Oh, isn't that lovely!" May I tell you, it's just like nothing compared to this Living Being that is meditating you. And that Living Being, and everyone's Living Being all united into one Being, forms the God that fell and fragmented Itself. And each fragment was perfect, and each fragment was the Father of the One meditating that one.

So, I tell you, try it here on this level. There is nothing in this world but God. This greatest of all confessions: "Hear, O Israel, the Lord our God, the Lord is one" . . that there aren't two of us . . not really, in the true sense of the word. But here, you take my word and test it here on this level in the world of Caesar. You want a better future? All right. Dare to take this statement and try it, but try it for this one week.

"I have assumed that I AM the one that I want to be. I AM still assuming that I AM it, and I will continue to assume that I AM it until that which I have assumed is objectively realized" . . and don't give it any time on this level. Just bear down on it, and dare to sleep in that assumption just as though it were true. Don't give it any time.

There is a time limit in what God, your own wonderful Father Who is in the depth of your own Being dreaming you . . He has that time limit; but on this level, there should not be lengths of time. You are told in Paul's letter to the Philippians:

"He who began a good work in you will bring it to completion at the day of Jesus Christ."

All right . . that will take its own good time. You will be brought to the same perfection of the Being who is dreaming you. It is God dreaming Himself into a greater expansion of Himself. That's all that it is. You are the Dreamer and the dream! You are not "another." You are the Dreamer and the dream. "He who began a good work in you will bring it to completion at the day of Jesus Christ." You'll find that in the 1st chapter, the 6th verse, of Philippians. So, you are the

Dreamer, dreaming yourself into the image of your Self. That's perfectly all right.

But while you are here, then take it in the world of Caesar and bring about these changes in your world for yourself and for those you love. Eventually you will love all, but if you don't love all now, do it at least for those that you do love, and actually assume it, and dare to say to yourself, "I have assumed it. I AM still assuming it. I will continue to assume it until what I have assumed, and still am assuming, is perfectly realized." For you are told, "Unless you believe that I AM He, you will die in your sins." Is someone talking to me? No. I am saying to myself, "Unless I believe I AM the Being I want to be, I die in my sins. I miss the mark." It's not another talking to me; there is only one God. There can't be two. And so, unless I believe I am that man that I want to be, then I remain as the man that I don't want to be; and therefore I "die in my sins." That is the story as told us in the 8th chapter of the book of John.

It's not another being telling me I must believe in him. Believe in what? I am not called upon to believe in any other being, for any other being is a false god. There's only one God. So, to believe in another . . I don't care who the other appears to be . . to believe in someone who calls himself the head of some great religious body . . whether it be Roman Catholicism, whether it be called Protestantism, whether it be called Judaism . . and to believe that he is the great leader, why, that's a false god. Unless I believe I AM He, I die in my sins. But I don't say that unless I believe that someone is talking to me who tells me unless I believe that he is something . . nonsense! That's all stupid. I don't believe that anyone else is. I must believe that God actually became me, that I may become God!

And so, His name is I AM. So, unless I believe that I am the man that I want to be, then I remain not being that man, and therefore die in my frustration . . and die in my sins. You get it? Sure you do.

So here, I tell you, try it. It may seem difficult, but it will not be difficult if you dare to "go out on a limb" and try it. You are this Being! There is only God. There is nothing but God. Let no one tell you that he is better than you are. There is no one in this world greater than you are! And if anyone dares to tell you that he is, turn your back on him and walk away. I don't care who he is . . or she is . . or they are. There is no one that is your superior, because you are God, and there is nothing but God in this world and God became you, that you may become God.

So, I admire the great, inspired poets. I do! I take Shakespeare and I read him and think, "Isn't this marvelous?" I take Blake. I can't quite follow the arguments of an Einstein . . no. But here are inspired men . . all of them: the Shakespeares, the Blakes, the Einsteins, and all the great painters in the world. But let no one tell you that these inspired men have some influx of Spirit that in any way whatsoever was greater than their own wonderful human imagination, because there is nothing greater than their own human imagination. It didn't come from something outside of themselves; it was their own imagination awakening. "And that same imagination is yours, because there is only one Spirit. There aren't two spirits.

So, the Spirit of Man is one with the Spirit of the Universe that sustains the whole vast world. That's the One Spirit. So, let no one tell you for one moment there is another spirit. There is no other spirit. So, tonight when you go home . . in fact, before you go, start it right here . . and this lovely, wonderful feeling. And may I tell you, I can't tell you what a joy it is to sleep in the assumption . . in the feeling . . that "I AM He."

All right, what comes in the course of the night . . what does it matter? May I tell you, when you slip into the deep, you come hurtling through all kinds of things between the depths of unconsciousness from this level and then waking; and in that one short interval you can have numberless crazy little dreams between the hurtling back from unconsciousness to this level. And you give importance to the little dream, based upon the surface as you are coming through. But you do not know what depths you reach in what is unconscious relative to this level.

So, let no one frighten you. You are an Immortal Being. You cannot die. You just cannot die! And if someone today has arrived at a certain point where it is seemingly before you did, it doesn't matter. He or she . . they are no better because they got there first. There is no "first." Everyone is coming into that level and when all . . and if they don't all come in, may I tell you, it isn't finished. And when all come in, the whole race is over. And what a rejoicing among all who formed the one Body! We are that Body . . that one spirit, that one body, that one lord, that one God and Father of all. There is nothing but God the Father. And everyone will prove to himself by the vision he is God the Father, and he does not resent anyone else being God the Father. How could he?

When Benny came home on Saturday, I can't tell you my thrill. Here is Benny . . and put us together. Let us put Benny on the stage right now. Our pigments are just as opposite as they can be, and we are the same Father of the same Child! I said, "Benny, tell me, what did he look like?" because we have fun together. It's not because we have martinis together. That comes, regardless. It was not because of any martinis. And I said, "Benny, what did he look like?"

He said, "Neville, he was the sweetest blonde . . this blue-eyed, blonde, fair-skinned lad, and here is my Son, and he is calling me 'Father,' and I knew I'm his father. And I so loved him . . I didn't care if the others left me, and left me with all these children. They are all my children anyway. I felt I was the father of all of them, but here was my Special One. Here was David!"

That's the same David that is my Son. Well now, he is the father of my son. Well, if he's the father of my son, are we not one? We are one! But on the surface, this strange, peculiar thing will be fighting each other because he is of a very, very dark skin and I am of an olive skin. Then people think, "Well, my god, they are different!" And it isn't so! In the depths of our Soul, we are one, because God is one. God is not multiple, He is made up of the many, but God is one.

The Story of Jesus Is Persistent Assumption

And when he tells me exactly how it happened, the thrill that is mine to see that he and I are one . . and he has the same child! That was the symbol of his "birth from above."

So, may I tell you? Go on. On this level of Caesar, apply this principle. Cushion yourself against the normal blows of the world. It's only natural. You want to be cushioned. You have a wife, a husband, children, friends who cannot cushion themselves because they don't believe it. But you love them to the point where you want to cushion them, regardless of whether they believe it or not.

So, they don't believe it. All right, then you cushion them anyway, because you love them. And you want to leave them enough money to give them a cushion. You aren't going to stop the depth of their own being from giving them blows, but you did your part in so loving them that you want to leave them a cushion. If you want to leave them a cushion in the world of Caesar, you leave them a little money; that's the cushion in this world.

So, what would it feel like if I could leave to those that I so love, say, a hundred thousand . . two hundred thousand? Now, what would it be like to depart this night just as though it meant nothing, and to leave them a quarter of a million, knowing that by tomorrow they may lose the whole thing? But that doesn't really matter. You did your part. You cushioned them for a moment, because the depth of their own being . . which is your own depth . . will simply take them through certain experiences to awaken them to the point where they are the Father of the one and only begotten Son of God. For all are searching for that one Son, to reveal to them the Cause of the phenomena, and the Cause is the Father, for the Father is one's Self.

Then one discovers, "Lord! I AM the only cause of the things that are happening to me in this world? There is not a thing in this world that has ever happened to me that I didn't cause it!" Well, what a responsibility! You mean I caused all the nonsense? Yes, I did. I mean, all the stupid things that happen to me? The blows? Yes. Well, then I've got to stop this peculiar silliness in my world!

Metaphysical / Law of Attraction Books

David Allen - The Power of I AM (2014), The Power of I AM - Volume 2 (2015), The Power of I AM - Volume 3 (2017)

David Allen - The Creative Power of Thought, Man's Greatest Discovery (2017)

David Allen - The Secrets, Mysteries & Powers of The Subconscious Mind (2017)

David Allen - The Money Bible - The Secrets of Attracting Prosperity (2017)

David Allen - Your Faith Is Your Fortune, Your Unlimited Power (2018)

David Allen - ASKffirmations: Questions That Create Reality

The Neville Goddard Collection (All 10 of his books plus 2 Lecture series) (2016)

Neville Goddard - Assumptions Harden Into Facts: The Book (2016)

Neville Goddard - Imagination: The Redemptive Power in Man (2016)

Neville Goddard - The World is At Your Command - The Very Best of Neville Goddard (2017)

Neville Goddard - Imagining Creates Reality - 365 Mystical Daily Quotes (2017)

Neville Goddard's Interpretation of Scripture (2018)

Neville Goddard - Consciousness, The Giver Of All Gifts (2019)

Neville Goddard - The Wish Fulfilled (2020)

Neville Goddard - The Story Of Jesus Is Persistent Assumption (2021)

The Definitive Christian D. Larson Collection (6 Volumes, 30 books) (2014)

David Allen - The Within Creates The Without: Creating Our Lives By Design: Daily Meditations

David Allen - The Creative Power Of Mind: Daily Meditations For A Better Life

Visit Us At **NevilleGoddardBooks.com** for a complete listing of all our books and **1000's of Free (mostly metaphysical) Books to Read online and or download.**

The most creative thing in us is to believe a thing into objective existence.

Neville Goddard

www.ingramcontent.com/pod-product-compliance
Lightning Source LLC
Chambersburg PA
CBHW030910080526
44589CB00010B/241